SUSTAINABLE DEVELOPMENT

Garrett Nagle & Kris Spencer

Hodder & Stoughton

A MEMBER OF THE HODDER HEADLINE GROUP

Acknowledgements

The authors would like to thank the following people: Christine Berry, Betty Morgan, Misia Newsome, Gill Yeomans and the Geography staff and students at St Edward's School, Oxford and St Paul's Girls' School, London.

The publishers would like to thank the following for giving permission to reproduce copyright photographs in this book: J Allan Cash, Figure 1.12; Associated Press, Figure 1.4; Bruce Coleman, Figure 7.7; Corbis, Figures 2.7 and 3.4; Sue Cunnigham, Figure 3.12; Life File, Figure 2.14; Panos Pictures, Figure 1.3.

All other photos supplied by Garrett Nagle.

All inside artwork by 1–11 Line Art.

British Library Cataloguing in Publication Data
A catalogue record for this title is available from The British Library

ISBN 0 340 67970 0

First published 1997
Impression number 10 9 8 7 6 5 4 3 2 1
Year   2002 2001 2000 1999 1998 1997

Typeset by Fakenham Photosetting Limited, Fakenham, Norfolk
Printed in Great Britain for Hodder & Stoughton Educational, a division of Hodder Headline Plc, 338 Euston Road, London NW1 3BH by Redwood Books, Trowbridge, Wiltshire.

For Rosie and Patrick; Tess and Cathy

Contents

1
SUSTAINABLE DEVELOPMENT

1.1 Introduction

Sustainable development is development which 'meets the needs of the present without compromising the ability of future generations to meet their own needs' (Brundtland, 1987). It is a process by which human potential (standard of well being) is improved and the environment (the resource base) is used and managed to supply humanity on a long-term basis. It implies social justice as well as long-term environmental sustainability. The definition suggests that mankind has degraded the planet and must make amends for future generations.

For some the term sustainable development is a catch phrase of 'beguiling simplicity' which is frequently used, but only as a form of lip service to environmentalists. Others claim that the term 'sustainable' is vague, emotive and ambiguous, as is the term 'development'. Sustainability is certainly popular: the EU has investigated the notion of 'sustainable economic and social development' since the Maastricht agreement; the World Bank is concerned with 'sustainable development and equitable development'; the IMF and OECD talk of 'sustainable economic growth'; and the UN Development Programme is committed to 'sustainable human development'.

1.2 World crises

The world is facing a number of interlinked crises which undermine the ability to achieve sustainable development. The United Nations Conference on the Environment and Development (the Earth Summit) held in Rio de Janeiro in 1992 and the Global Forum in Manchester, 1994 warned that unless there were changes in the ways in which development proceeded, there would be a large increase in the amount of human suffering and environmental damage. The crises encompass social, economic, environmental and political aspects.

Currently about one-fifth of the world's 5.8 billion population live in desperately poor conditions – these are the global 'underclass'. Their lives are at the edge of existence and are continuously close to famine, disease, hunger and death. Since the 1960s political and economic changes in the global order have made some less economically developed countries (LEDCs) even poorer compared with the more economically developed countries (MEDCs) (Figure 1.1). Urban regions have grown at the expense of rural areas

and the poorest are constrained by a lack of power and control over their own destiny. Within the underclass certain groups are more vulnerable than others: in particular, women, children and indigenous people. In an ordinary year 14 million children under the age of five die in LEDCs. During wars, famines, plagues, economic recession and other disasters the number increases.

1960	30:1
1970	32:1
1980	45:1
1989	59:1
1991	61:1

FIGURE 1.1 Changing ratios of richest 20 per cent and poorest 20 per cent (by income) since 1960

The United Nations Population Conference in Cairo, 1994, set out plans to stabilise the world's population at about 10 billion. Some places, notably China, India and south east Asia, which account for 40 per cent of the world's population, are experiencing unprecedented economic growth. The implications of this for environmental degradation are clear. In other parts the crises are different: in MEDCs unemployment and recession pose grave problems for sustainable development. By contrast in the former Soviet Union, economic stagnation, poverty and a legacy of environmental dereliction impose severe constraints on the success of any sustainable programme.

The environmental crisis is a result of the limited amount of resources that the earth contains and the rate at which they are being destroyed (Figure 1.2). Moreover, there is a social aspect to the destruction of resources: the 20 per cent of the world's population that live in MEDCs consume 80 per cent of the world's resources whereas the 80 per cent of the population that live in LEDCs use only 20 per cent of the resources. Since many of the resources that are consumed in MEDCs come from LEDCs, much of the cost of resource depletion is paid for by LEDCs. Resources are not only consumed. Some are degraded through pollution and misuse. The pattern and causes are complex. For example, desertification affects up to a third of the world, and is increasing. The range of factors which have been linked to it is large and includes population growth, climatic change, intensification of farming, resettlement of nomads, provision of boreholes, development of schools and health facilities, removal of trees, lack of fuelwood and government policies for taxation and conscription.

FIGURE 1.2 Selected environmental problems

- 70 per cent of the world's drylands are degraded
- desertification costs $42 million a year
- 39 per cent of NPP (net primary productivity) by plants on land is lost by people each year
- the amount of farmland has fallen from 0.38 ha/person in 1970 to 0.28 in 1990 and at current rates will reach 0.15 in the year 2050
- fish catches in all of the world's 17 fisheries areas exceed sustainable limits

FIGURE 1.3 (top right) Refugee camp in Rwanda

FIGURE 1.4 (bottom right) Oil wells on fire after the Gulf War

The world's environmental crises are increasingly rapid, and cross international boundaries. For example, the transfer of radioactive waste and acid rain across Western Europe, and the build up of greenhouse gases in the atmosphere, cross international and terrestrial boundaries. The causes of the crises are changing: for example in the early part of the century greenhouse gases were linked to coal-burning industries and now are generally blamed on the phenomenon of mass private car ownership. Since 1900 the world's population has tripled and industrial production increased 50 fold. Some 80 per cent of industrial production has taken place since 1950. However, the trend is not irreversible: the 1956 Clean Air Act of Britain and the cleaning of the River Thames in the 1970s and 1980s show that environments can be improved on a long term basis with proper planning.

Political conflict in the form of war, ethnic cleansing, refugee crises, trading blocs, trade wars and economic sanctions have increased. In the early 1990s there were conflicts and renewed violence in Somalia, Ethiopia, Sudan, Rwanda, Burundi, Kuwait, Nigeria, Croatia, Bosnia, Serbia, Chechnya, Israel, Sri Lanka and Northern Ireland among others.

These crises interact and reinforce each other. It makes the task of sustainable development much more difficult. For example, the prospects for sustainable tourism in Northern Ireland vary with political changes and with the status of the IRA ceasefire. On the other hand, political change in South Africa has reduced population pressure in some dryland areas and improved the prospects for sustainable dryland agriculture. It has also boosted the hopes for sustainable ecotourism. Any detailed analysis of sustainable options show that political change, economic development, environmental impact and social justice cannot be separated. Each of these aspects needs to be addressed if sustainable development is to occur.

Student Activity 1.1

1 What other types of development are there other than sustainable development? How is sustainable development different from them?

2 In the passage above it is implied that economic growth in south east Asia will have a serious impact upon the environment.

a Explain at least **two** reasons why economic

growth in south east Asia in the 1990s will differ from that in Britain and Germany in the late nineteenth and early twentieth centuries.
b What implications does this have for the environment and sustainable development.
3 a To what extent do you think sustainable development can be carried out at
(i) a local
(ii) a national and
(iii) an international level?
Give examples to illustrate your answer.
b To what extent can sustainable development be a top-down process? Give reasons for your answer.

4 Discuss how far it is possible to talk about sustainable development when we do not know what the needs of the future generations will be.
5 'We live in a world dominated by market forces. Sustainable development must fit into this.'
a Give examples of how 'market forces' influence the type and nature of development that occurs in a named location.
b How far do you agree that sustainable development must fit into this system? Give reasons for your answer.
c What implications does this have for the natural environment?

1.3   *Modelling man and the environment*

Simple models have long been used by geographers to show the relationship between carrying capacity (how many people, or how much use, the environment can hold) and population growth (or resource exploitation) (Figure 1.5).
1 Continuous growth may occur if there are huge resources or growing resources.
2 Sigmoid (S-shaped) growth occurs when societies react before a crisis occurs or a resource is exhausted.
3 Over-exploitation and readjustment occur when societies react after a disaster and the environment is given time to recover. Resource exploitation becomes progressively fine-tuned with resource availability and sustainability.
4 Over-exploitation and collapse occur if the resource cannot be replaced (finite resources) and society does not take any sustainable precautions.

One of the earliest of the 'new generation' of models which examined the impact of people on the earth's environment was Kenneth Boulding, a British economist based in the USA. In 1966 he popularised the concept of 'spaceship earth' and provided two scenarios for economic development. The first was the 'robber-' or 'cowboy-economy' with unlimited growth and no checks on conservation. Success was measured in terms of industrial output and there was little thought for the long-term future of the planet. Global catastrophe resulted. The other idea was to see the world as a 'spaceship-economy', a closed system, with limited resources and ultimately dependent upon the solar ecosystem. In this economy mankind has to work with the system, conserve resources and plan for future survival. Long-term stability could be achieved this way.

The spectre of rapid population growth and resource depletion prompted Garret Hardin to write *The Tragedy of the Commons* (1986). His idea is simple but crucial. If each individual that has a right of access and use to a common resource – whether it is a meadow, forest or mineral resource – continues

to increase his yield to improve his standard of living relative to the other, the stock will eventually become depleted. All those that depend upon it, including that individual, will suffer as a result. The analogy with global economic growth is clear. Hardin reached the conclusion that the use of resources must be governed by some authority, be it scientific, political, land-owning etc. This begs the questions *Who supervises the supervisors?*

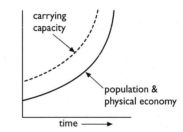

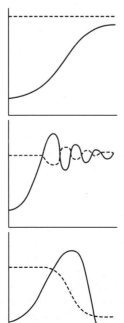

FIGURE 1.5 Possible relationship between population growth and carrying capacity

1.4 The Limits to Growth

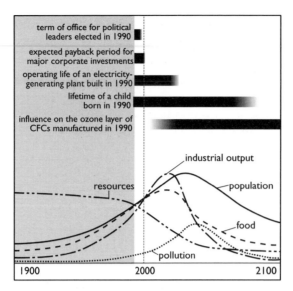

FIGURE 1.6 The original limits to growth

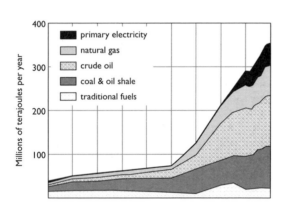

FIGURE 1.7 World energy use

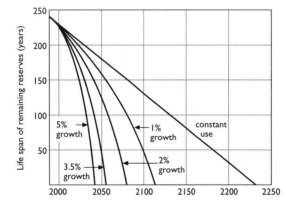

FIGURE 1.8 Depletion of the World's gas reserves assuming different rates of growth in consumption

FIGURE 1.9 (far right) Sustainable limits to growth

The *Limits to Growth* was a report prepared for the Club of Rome. It painted a pessimistic picture about the state of the world's resources and the likelihood of resource degradation. It concluded that the limits to growth on this planet would occur within one hundred years. They forecast a severe fall in industrial output and food supplies around 2010 and a rapid decline in population around 2050 (Figure 1.6). Pollution was seen as one of the main causes of the collapse of the system. Increasing resource consumption was also a problem. For example, trends in energy use were clearly linked with the rise in technology. Not only was more energy being used up, at an accelerating or exponential rate, but the type of energy resource was also changing (Figure 1.7). By the late 1980s less than 50 years' worth of oil reserves remained; and if consumption of gas continues to grow at its present rate of 3.5 per cent per annum an amount of gas equal to four times the known reserves would be used up by the year 2054 (Figure 1.8)! Others argue that oil supply, for example, has always been based on continuous exploration and development, and new discoveries have always been made to replace those depleted. New technologies such as horizontal drilling and enhanced oil recovery have enabled engineers to extract more oil from existing resources. The report was criticised on a number of counts most notably the lack of a regional dimension and the absence of any measures to manage or solve the impending disaster. Nevertheless, the basic message was, and is, correct: the earth cannot sustain economic growth which depends upon an increasing amount of resource consumption.

In the original *Limits to Growth* (1972) society developed without any major changes in policies relating to resource exploitation. Population and industry grow until a combination of environmental and resource constraints prevent further growth.

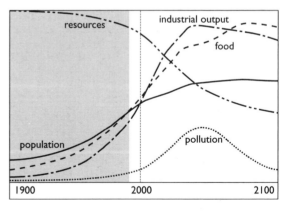

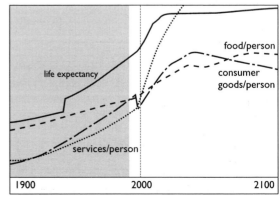

Investment declines, old industrial capital deteriorates, pollution increases, food production falls and there is a decline in life expectancy.

In a re-run of the model the authors build in a number of new scenarios. These include a variety of factors and situations (on a global scale) such as:

■ deliberate constraints on population growth;
■ trade-offs between population size and levels of material well-being;
■ technologies to conserve resources;
■ increased farming efficiency;
■ reductions in the levels of pollution;
■ the rates of renewable resources do not exceed their rates of regeneration;
■ the rates of use of non-renewable resources do not exceed the rate at which sustainable renewable substitutes are developed;
■ the rates of pollution do not exceed the tolerance of the environment.

With these changes it is possible to see a very different pattern from the one drawn in 1972 (Figure 1.9).

Student Activity 1.2

1 Study the list of ways of achieving sustainable growth.

   a What are the issues connected with the deliberate constraint on population growth?

   b Briefly explain how farming efficiency can be improved. What are the associated costs of making farming more efficient?

   c Describe and explain how a named sustainable substitute has been developed to replace a non-renewable resource. What, if any, are the geographic issues of the development of this resource?

1.5   Beyond the Limits to Growth

In the early 1970s the Ecologist magazine published *Blueprint for survival* written by the same authors who wrote the *Limits to Growth*. The report predicted that without change there would be a breakdown in society and irreversible environment degradation by the end of the twentieth century. Growth creates growth, they argued, for a number of reasons:

■ industrial growth led to population growth and this in turn created demand for more growth (cumulative causation);
■ economic growth reduced the risk of unemployment;

■ growth is needed for profits which are needed for investment;
■ the success of governments is often measured in growth-related indicators;
■ recession leads to social and political instability.

However, in *Blueprint* they outlined some of the requirements for a stable, sustainable society:
■ minimum disruption to ecological processes;
■ increased conservation of resources;
■ zero population growth;
■ a just social system.

1.6   Recent developments

The World Commission on Environment and Development 1987

The World Commission on Environment and Development (WCED) chaired by Brundtland investigated the capacity of the earth to support its population and the ways in which human activities were affecting the environment. These activities have created crises of environment, development, security and energy.

The Brundtland Commission's concept of sustainable development has two key aspects:
■ the achievement of basic needs for all people, especially the global underclass;
■ limits to growth are technical, cultural and social. This is in stark contrast to the Meadows' idea that the limits to growth were environmental and resource availability. Brundtland's analysis contains

a belief that equity, growth and environmental sustainability are simultaneously possible and that countries will want to work towards that goal.

Brundtland suggested seven major proposals for a strategy for sustainable development:
■ revive economic growth;
■ change the quality of growth;
■ meet basic needs of food, water, employment, energy and sanitation;
■ stabilise population growth;
■ conserve and enhance resources;
■ adapt technology to manage risk;
■ put environment into economics.

The Brundtland Commission reported to the United Nations General Assembly, which in turn requested a five-year progress report. This became the Rio conference, the largest ever environmental conference.

United Nations Conference on Environment and Development, 1992 (UNCED)

The outcomes of Rio were:
■ convention on biodiversity;
■ framework convention on climatic change;
■ principles of forest management;
■ Agenda 21;
■ the Rio Declaration on Environment and Development.

The *Convention on biodiversity* is a legally binding document which seeks to conserve biodiversity, species and ecosystems. UNEP estimate that there may be up to 30 million species in the world, of which only 1.5 million have been described and up to 25 per cent of the total may face extinction. Up to 100 species a day may become extinct. One hundred and fifty five countries signed. However, some MEDCs, such as the USA, refused to sign as they feared it would restrict their biotechnology industry. Others believed it was a way of making MEDCs pay for the preservation of ecosystems in LEDCs such as the Amazonian rainforest. Some of the benefits are shown in Figure 1.6.

FIGURE 1.10 Some benefits of biodiversity

> ■ In Boston Harbour, retaining natural salt marshes saves up to $17 million each year in flood protection works
> ■ In Zimbabwe, the CAMPFIRE project, (Communal Areas Management For Indigenous REsources) has shown that cropping of wild species yields more than land converted to ranching
> ■ Agro-forestry uses a greater proportion of rainforest species without increasing the risks of environmental deterioration, e.g. the Popolucan Indians in the Santa Rosa district of Mexico
> ■ Traditional herbalists provide primary health care to over two million people annually
> ■ Plant derived drugs have a commercial value of over $43 billion in 1985
> ■ Simple genes derived from Ethiopian Barley protect California's $160 million barley crop from the yellow dwarf virus

The *Framework Convention on climatic change* was signed by 153 countries. MEDCs agreed to stabilise their emissions of greenhouse gases to 1990 levels. LEDCs argued that they should not be prevented from developing and therefore had to fuel rapid economic growth. Only Germany and the UK have been successful in reducing their emissions. The UK hopes to be between 4 and 8 per cent below 1990 emissions by the year 2000. How far this is a result of environmental sentiment is questionable. Instead it reflects declining coal industries and a shift to a post-industrial society.

The *Principles of forest management* and the *Rio Declaration on Environment and Development* appeared to be well meaning but unachievable statements, partly on account of their sheer scale and content. By contrast, *Agenda 21* was a detailed document which spelt out a programme for sustainable development. Four main groups were considered:
1 Social and economic development – international cooperation, poverty, population, health, settlements;
2 Resource management – atmosphere, land resource planning, deforestation, mountains, fragile ecosystems, biodiversity, biotechnology, waste disposal;
3 Strengthening the participation of major groups – vulnerable peoples, NGOs, local, national and international governments;
4 Means of implementation – finance, institutions, technology transfer, education.

Role of local Agenda 21

As a result of the Earth Summit national governments are obliged to formulate national plans or strategies for sustainable development – *Agenda 21*. According to Timberlake (quoted in Elliot, 1994) it is people who do development, not governments, and therefore sustainable development is a local activity. Moreover, according to Chambers (1983) all people, however poor, have some ability, however constrained, of changing what they do, in small ways.

Local authorities are beginning to translate the global sustainability agenda into local action. Just as global sustainability cannot exist without national sustainable policies, national *Agenda 21* is incomplete without local *Agenda 21*.

Local authorities have a number of roles in sustainable development:
■ as a consumer of resources;
■ as a force for change in the market place;
■ as a role model for other organisations;
■ as providers of information;
■ as providers of services;
■ as planners;
■ as local governments and decision makers.

1.7 Agenda 21 in practice: environmental issues in Chiang Mai, Thailand

Chiang Mai is an important tourist location in the north of Thailand, 750 km from Bangkok (Figure 1.11). It covers an area of approximately 40 km² and has a population of 163 568. Chiang Mai acts as a regional centre for trade, economic development, education, tourism and service provision in northern Thailand. Urbanisation and urban sprawl are both occurring at an alarming speed. The issues raised in Chiang Mai illustrate some of the potentials and constraints that city authorities face in their attempt to improve the environment.

The main problems that are experienced in Chiang Mai include short-term problems such as water pollution, drainage, solid waste disposal and air pollution. These have been referred to as the 'brown agenda'. In addition, there are long-term problems to do with traffic and transport, new buildings and the preservation of historic-cultural buildings, shanty town improvements and land-use management and planning.

The Mae Ping River, which passes through Chiang Mai, is the main source of water for the city,

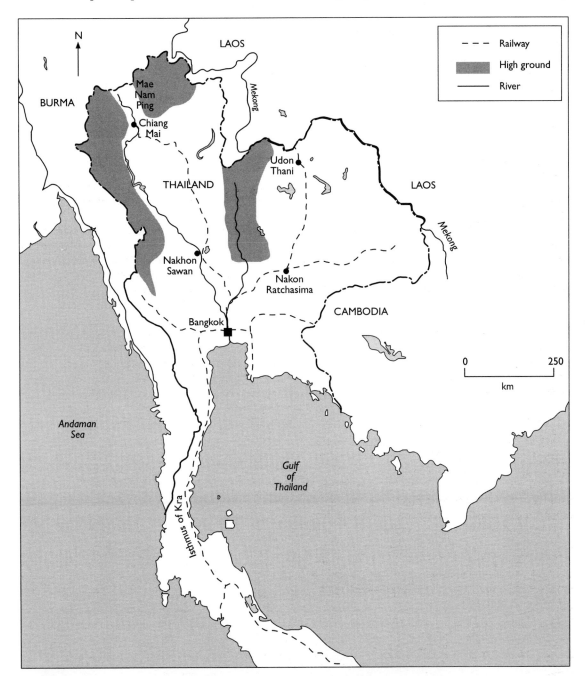

FIGURE 1.11 Location of Chiang Mai, Thailand

but it is heavily polluted due to the large number of buildings close to it which are lacking in any form of proper sanitation. Moreover, large-scale floods occur, on average, every other year, as a result of heavy monsoon rains. The Chiang Mai Municipal Council has proposed a sewage system to run alongside the river, a sewage treatment plant to tackle the worst affected areas and improvements to the limited existing drainage systems.

Air pollution is a major problem in Chiang Mai. This is partly due to the city's location, surrounded by mountains. Under high pressure conditions, still air is trapped and becomes heavily polluted with a cocktail of carbon monoxide, nitrogen oxide and photochemical ozone. In the city alone there are over 100 000 registered vehicles. The problem is compounded by individual refuse burning, farmers burning rice straw and grass, and the lighting of fire crackers for the festivals. Most people use sheets of foam to make their floats for festivals, and this material can only be disposed of by burning. The authorities have attempted to reduce the problem with a two-pronged approach. First, an educational programme to increase awareness about the environmental effects of burning substances such as foam, and suggestions that people use other materials such as banana leaves and bark. Secondly, a new incinerator and land-fill site have been proposed although there has been little development over the problem of insufficient refuse collection.

In Chiang Mai a combination of narrow roads, insufficient parking spaces and pavement traders is increasing the traffic congestion problem caused by large-scale ownership of private vehicles. The authorities plan to improve the mass transit system or public transport, computerise traffic signals and increase some road sizes.

The City Authorities have also had some impact in land-use management and planning. Part of the problem was the speed with which buildings were erected, the lack of any effective planning control and the inappropriate development of the urban area. Since 1985, the Chiang Mai city planning by-law has created separate areas for industrial, commercial, government, residential, religious and recreational land-uses. Conservation areas have also been created in the city in which no factory, cinema or billboard may be located adjacent to old temples, and no building should be over 12 m in height. In addition, all new buildings should have a traditional Lanna-Thai roof style.

Development in the past was hampered by the lack of effective planning controls. Now Chiang Mai has developed guidelines for managing the environment which involve local people, government organisations and non-government organisations (NGOs) in a way that allows for local and national political views and environmental and economic issues to be considered.

Student Activity 1.3

1 What are the main causes of Chiang Mai's environmental problems?
2 Are Chiang Mai's problems typical of most cities in the developing world? Explain your answer with reference to other examples.
3 How do the problems of London (23–4) compare with those of Chiang Mai?
4 How far can London and Chiang Mai be considered as 'sustainable cities'. Which do you think is the most suitable and why?

FIGURE 1.12 Chiang Mai, Thailand

2
POPULATION AND RESOURCES

2.1 Introduction

Nearly one billion people will be added to the planet during the 1990s. Even though birth rates are declining in almost every country the number of young women reaching child-bearing age is larger than ever before. This means the number of babies will go on rising even though birth rates have fallen. Eighty per cent of the world's population lives in the developing world and this growth will put pressure on renewable resources such as water, land and fuelwood because:

■ more water will be needed for rapidly expanding cities;
■ forests will need to be cleared for agricultural land;
■ farmers will be forced on to steep land, leading to soil erosion.

This chapter identifies the problems and opportunities associated with sustainable development in an increasingly overcrowded world.

2.2 Population growth trends

The United Nations Population Fund (UNFPA) predicts that the World's population will be over 8.5 billion by 2025 and that it may eventually level off between 10 to 12 billion. Ninety five per cent of this growth will be in Developing Countries (Figure 2.1). The largest increase will be in Southern Asia where numbers will rise from 1.2 billion to 1.5 billion by the end of the century. Over the same period Africa's 650 million will rise to 900 million. In contrast Europe's population will hardly change at all. However, countries in the Developed World will face problems of sustainability based on an ageing population.

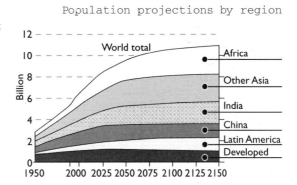

FIGURE 2.1 The rise of World population

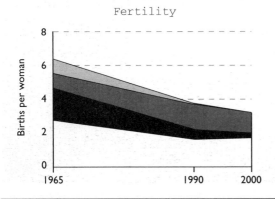

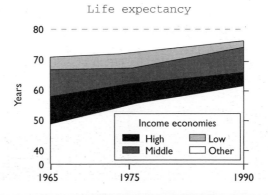

FIGURE 2.2 Human induced imbalances

Theory	Explanation
Neo-Malthusian	Demographic pressure leads to overuse and inappropriate use of resources
Ignorance	Ignorance of the workings of nature means that mistakes are made, leading to unintended consequences
Tragedy of the commons	Overuse or misuse of certain resources occurs because they are commonly owned
Poor valuation	Overuse or misuse of certain resources occurs because they are not properly valued in economic terms
Dependency	Inappropriate resource use by certain groups is encouraged or compelled by the influence of more powerful groups
Exploitation	Overuse and misuse of resources is pursued deliberately by a culture driven by consumerism
Human domination over nature	Environmental issues result from human misapprehension of being above rather than part of nature

There are two major debates which are at the heart of population and development:
(i) Is the world overcrowded?
(ii) Are current lifestyles sustainable?
Figure 2.2 shows a number of theories which link population growth to environmental problems.

Why might an environmentalist disagree with this concept of 'optimum' population?

FIGURE 2.3 Four generations of a Japanese family in Tokyo

Student Activity 2.1

1 Figure 2.4 shows a simple diagram explaining the concept of under, over and optimum-population.
  a How are the terms related to population density, level of technological development and resources.
  b A country may have a very low population density but still be over-populated. Explain this statement.
  c In many ways optimum population is an economic construct. It suggests that resources can be fully exploited to the benefit of society at large.

FIGURE 2.4 Under, over and optimum population

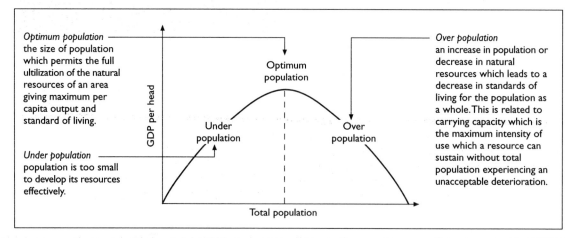

Optimum population – the size of population which permits the full ultilization of the natural resources of an area giving maximum per capita output and standard of living.

Under population – population is too small to develop its resources effectively.

Over population – an increase in population or decrease in natural resources which leads to a decrease in standards of living for the population as a whole. This is related to carrying capacity which is the maximum intensity of use which a resource can sustain without total population experiencing an unacceptable deterioration.

GDP per head

Optimum population

Under population

Over population

Total population

2 Figure 2.5 shows the relationship between population growth and renewable resources. Many scientists suggest that earth has a 'carrying capacity' beyond which ecosystems cannot cope with further increases.

a What is a renewable resource?

b Do you agree that the world has a carrying capacity (a maximum number of people it can support)?

c What would be the result of exceeding the carrying capacity of each of the resources shown in Figure 2.5?

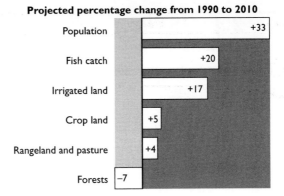

FIGURE 2.5 Population change and renewable resources

2.3 *Views of Population Growth*

```
1.  Neo Malthusian (Ehrlich)
        increased population
                ↓
        increased demand for
        food and resources
                ↓
        less food per person
                ↓
        increased mortality      →  decrease in
                ↓                    population growth
        decreased fertility
```

Expanding population means increasing food production causing environmental and financial problems.

```
2.  Resource Optimists/Cornucopians (Simon,
Boserup)
        increased population
                ↓
        increased demand for food
                ↓
        improvements in technology
                ↓
        resources can now sustain      increase in
        a larger population        →   population
```

People are the ultimate resource – through innovation or intensification humans can respond to increased numbers.

The effects of continued population growth on the environment and the quality of human life seem clear: more people will use more resources and as these resources are finite there will be fewer of them to go round. And yet there are many who argue that the human race is the ultimate resource. Figure 2.6 shows these two opposing viewpoints:

■ the neo-Malthusians have developed from a view that the world cannot feed its rapidly increasing population to a more moderate view that coping with providing extra food will lead to environmental problems and a lack of investment in development especially in less developed countries;

■ the resource optimists argue that increased population leads to a rise in standards of living; only when populations begin to increase is there the stimulus for technological development.

FIGURE 2.6 (left top and bottom) Models of population and resources

---

Student Activity 2.2

FIGURE 2.7 Lyndon Johnson

1 In the 1960s Lyndon Johnson, the then US President, argued that $5 spent on family planning was just as effective in promoting development as $100 invested in increasing agricultural or industrial production.

a Do you agree with this viewpoint? Give reasons for your answer.

b What are the arguments against strictly enforced family planning?

2.4   Is the World Overcrowded?

The traditional debate between the neo-Malthusians (population growth is bad) and the resource optimists (the world can cope with ever increasing numbers) is mirrored in the growing divide between environmentalists (resources should be conserved and protected) and economists (resources should be exploited).

These arguments are of tremendous importance when linking population growth to sustainable development. But there is another way of viewing the relationship between population, resources and development. In this case the issue is not the numbers of people but rather the amount of resources they consume per head. This leads to a number of interesting ideas:

- the West is over populated in terms of what it consumes;
- in the Developing World a colonial past has led to an uneven relationship with the West which has led to increased poverty and an exploitation of the developing world's resources.

These ideas have been linked to the theory of uneven developments.

FIGURE 2.8 (right)

Uneven development

Uneven development means that the experience of rapid population growth has been very different between the Developed and Developing World. Countries in the Developed World have high incomes and high levels of technological development. This means they can react quickly to environmental problems with 'technological fixes'. In the Developing World lack of capital means these technological fixes are not as easy to implement. Uneven development also means that the west has already degraded much of its environment.

> - Twenty three per cent of Europe's land is degraded
> - Seventy five per cent of all CO_2 emissions are generated by the developed world

Student Activity 2.3

Figure 2.9 shows the impact of European development on the world.
1 In what ways did colonial expansion in the nineteenth century cause problems for the developing world in the twentieth century?
2 Account for uneven development on the world scale.

FIGURE 2.9 The impact of Europe on the World and the creation of uneven development

Nineteenth Century
- outmigration acted as a 'safety valve' for expanding population
- concept of developing world as a 'wilderness' which should be colonisation
- population decline of indigenous peoples
- plural society created

- legal and political control
- raw materials used for European industry
- cumulative causation leads to primacy
- export finished products to 'Third World' markets

Twentieth Century
- depressed prices for raw materials of third world countries
- best land is used to produce luxury food for export to the west
- surplus food given as 'aid' depresses prices for local farmers

- environmental problems of the world are due to the 'overconsumption of the west'
- the preservation of 'wilderness' in the developing world is an issue in the west because our natural areas are gone
- export of 'brown' industries to developing world
- MNCs exploit developing worlds mining resources leading to pollution

emigration   trade

Impact of Europe on the World

colonialism   pollution

2.5 The role of women in development

Population pressure coupled with the effects of uneven development have led to environmental and development crises in many developing world regions. The need for sustainable development in these areas is being increasingly linked to the role of women in society. Women in many developing world countries have an important position in rural communities, where they perform three crucial roles:

■ they are reproducers controlling birth rates and managing the domestic sphere;
■ they are producers contributing labour to growing crops;
■ they are community managers contributing to projects as varied as road building to the maintenance of clinics and schools.

Policy makers are increasingly recognising the role of women in economic and social development. The UN set up two organisations, UNIFEM and the International Research and Training Institute for the Advancement of Women (INSTRAW). By 1981 there were 60 international women's NGOs. These organisations recognise two things:

■ women's rights need to be improved in many countries in the Developing World (education, access to contraception, status);
■ women are the ground level decision makers capable of implementing policies of sustainable development.

Figure 2.10 summarises the attitude towards women in development over the last 20 years.

Student Activity 2.4

---

1 Use Figure 2.10 to describe the change in the way women are perceived in the development process over the period 1970–90.
2 Why do you think the policies of equity and empowerment were unpopular with national governments?

Case Study: Women's Horticultural Production in The Gambia – The Sukuta Women's Co-operative Project

Women in rural Africa are major contributors to agricultural production. In Gambia it is estimated that women produce 80 per cent of the food grown, processed and eaten. Women also have the responsibility of securing household fuelwood and water, as well as caring for small stock. All these tasks are dependent on the careful and conscious maintenance of environmental resources.

The Sukuta Women's Co-operative Project is an example of a scheme which has tried to improve the conditions for women in two ways: income generation and labour-saving devices.

FIGURE 2.10 The different policy approaches to women in Africa over the last 20 years

Issues	Welfare	Equity	Anti Poverty	Efficiency	Empowerment
Period most popular	1950–70	1975–85	1970s onward	post 1980s	1975 onward
Purpose	women are given the resources to become better mothers	to gain equity for women in the development process; women seen as active participants in the development	a toned-down equity programme; women's poverty seen as a problem of under-development not of subordination	to ensure development is more efficient and more effective; women's economic participation is linked to equity	to empower women through greater self reliance: women's subordination and colonial oppression
Needs of women met and roles recognised	food aid and family planning	reduction of inequality with men by allowing political and economic autonomy	allows women to earn an income in small-scale income generating projects	relies on the three roles of women to replace declining social services	bottom-up role is recognised as women are empowered in terms of their triple role
Comment	women are seen in their traditional reproductive roles; little change of status	in identifying subordinate role of women, criticised as western feminism and not popular with governments	poor women isolated as a separate category; popular with small-scale NGOs	women seen entirely in terms of delivery capacity and ability to extend working day	emphasis on self-reliance; largely unsupported at present

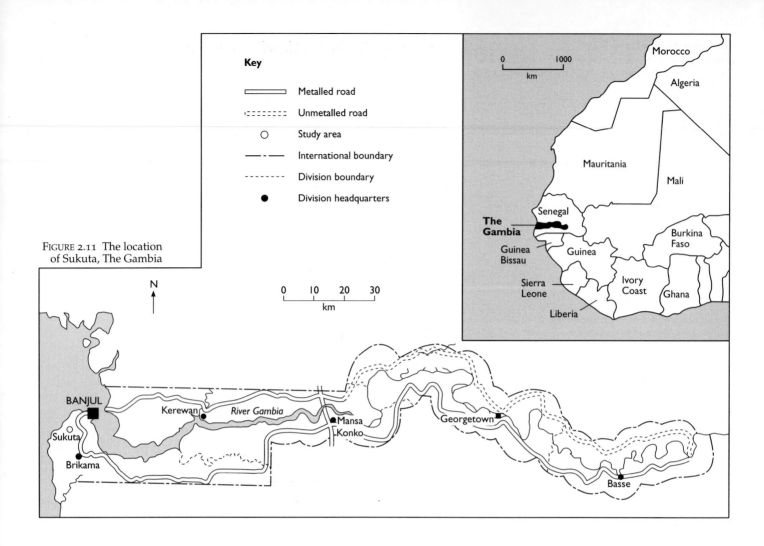

FIGURE 2.11 The location of Sukuta, The Gambia

Key

Metalled road	
Unmetalled road	
○	Study area
International boundary	
Division boundary	
●	Division headquarters

The Scheme

Figure 2.11 shows the location of Sukuta, a village where a high technology approach was introduced to increase the carrying capacity of the area by promoting horticulture. The women's communal garden project at Sukuta was set up in June 1987 and funded by the Islamic Development Bank (IDB). Figure 2.12 reveals some of the changes which were implemented. The scheme certainly made life easier for women but the sustainability of this high technology solution has been questioned.

(a) Environmental sustainability

The tree-felling which underpins the scheme has potentially damaging effects on the environment. The high temperatures on bare soil surfaces (in excess of 60°C on sandy loam) leads to oxidation of humus reducing organic matter and the water holding capacity of the soil. The lack of trees also means there is less protection against high intensity rainfall which leads to soil erosion.

FIGURE 2.12 Comparison between traditional horticultural methods and the Sukuta scheme

Traditional	Sukuta scheme
■ low technology	■ high technology
■ concrete lined wells where water is drawn by buckets	■ borehole sunk with electrical pump lifting water to the surface
■ laborious lifting and watering by hand	■ spray irrigation using electrical water pump
■ women working 36 hours a week on horticultural plots which are unfunded	■ women spend an average 12 hours per week in the horticultural scheme
■ tree cover valued in retaining soil moisture by shade	■ tree cover removed to enable spray irrigation

(b) Economic sustainability
The funding of the scheme by the IDB only lasted for two years. The scheme has created a number of problems.
■ the total annual cost of the scheme is over £2500 per year but the potential for profit is only £1500 per year
■ too many members had enrolled in the scheme and the membership had to be cut from 448 to 230
■ there is no back-up for the diesel pump so if it fails fields cannot be irrigated
The scheme looks likely to fail. The motives were well intentioned but this top-down technology-fix is clearly unsuitable in both economic and environmental terms.

Student Activity 2.5

1 The Sukuta Scheme suggests that a technology fix is often inappropriate to the needs of women. Need this always be the case? Give reasons for your answer.
2 Use Figure 2.12 to suggest the advantages and disadvantages of both methods.

Case Study: 'The Kerala Model' – Women in Public Action

Kerala is a largely agricultural state situated in the southwest corner of India. As a state it is the most densely populated area of India but with an even spread of population and no big cities. It has had remarkable success in improving health, literacy and education, and in bringing down the birth rate. Its success is even more remarkable because it has a much lower per capita income than the rest of India. Figure 2.13 shows just how much Kerala has achieved.

Three factors have been suggested to account for Kerala's success:
■ the autonomy and stability of its left wing coalition government;
■ long standing and continuing social reform;
■ the status of women in society.
The result is a society which has enabled large sections of the population to give voice to their views and needs.

	Kerala	India	Upper middle-income countries*
GNP per capita (US$)	<200	290*	1890
Crude birth rate	22.4	33.6	27.0
Crude death rate	6.2	11.9	8.0
Total fertility rate	2.1	4.4*	3.5
Infant mortality rate	27	96	50
Maternal mortality rate	1.3	3.5	1.2
Life expectancy at birth			
(male)	67	55	64
(female)	70	54	70
Sex-ratio (women per 1000 men)	1032	931	
Literacy rate†	70.0	36.0	
(male)	75.0	47.0	
(female)	66.0	25.0	
Population per registered doctor	1994*	2529*	1380*

FIGURE 2.13 Social development indicators for Kerala, 1989

[Data sources: Government of Kerala, 1989; World Band, 1989; Census of India, 1981]
* 1989 data
† 1981 data

The role of women

The status of women in the society of Kerala has been tremendously important in the region's development:
■ there is a tradition of female education whereby girls are educated to the same standard as boys;
■ also there is open access to universities and colleges where women often study to be nurses and doctors;
■ jobs opened up for educated women in health and education departments in the early twentieth century;

FIGURE 2.14 Women
working in the
developing world

■ women have autonomy in personal life where
there is no tradition of dowries and no obstacles to
remarriage.

All these factors coupled with a tradition of
matrilineal inheritance means that women are not
dependent on their husbands and girl children are
welcome. The result is a society where women take
responsibility for health care, and are able to seek
prompt medical advice. This is a bottom up
approach to health care: women determine their
own health needs. The result has been accelerated
family planning which women accept because the
health of their children is assured. Life is still very
hard for women in Kerala. The fishing villages on
the coast are overcrowded and here the mortality
rates are much higher. The model does show,
however, that if women are enabled and given what
they want, the results can be impressive.

Student Activity 2.6

1 Kerala's success is based on social development
rather than economic development. What
advantages are there to a system which places
public health and education ahead of
industrialisation?

2 Kerala's system developed over many years.
Would it be possible to use the same model in other
areas?

3
URBANISATION

3.1 Introduction

The Agenda 21 pledges made at the Rio summit have given rise to two further global meetings about the sustainable development of urban areas. In June 1994 representatives from 50 cities met in Manchester at Global Forum. Two years later, world representatives met again in Istanbul under the guise of the Habitat II conference.

The links between sustainability and a rise in population have already been discussed in Chapter Two. Population pressure is often linked to the deterioration of rural areas with respect to overgrazing, soil degradation and deforestation. But it can be argued that the major problems of the world's rising population will be felt in urban areas, both in the Developed and Developing World. In the west the question is 'How can the well being of future urban populations be assured with a more frugal use of resources?' In the Developing World questions deal with more basic needs like providing housing, sanitation and health care for an ever increasing urban population. Every city in the world must deal with the congestion and pollution caused by the motor car. Cities must also educate their residents, industrialists, commuters and planners to pollute less and recycle more.

3.2 The rise of the megacity

According to the British Charity, Population Concern, by the year 2000, over half of the world's population will live in megacities of over 10 million people. The growth of urban areas is particularly important in the Developing World where between 20 million and 30 million people are moving to towns and cities each year.

Megacities look set to grow from 12 in 1996 to 25 by the turn of the century and 33 by 2015, 21 of which will be in Asia.

FIGURE 3.1 Shanty town housing in Ndevana

Student Activity 3.1

1 In the past, urban expansion was evenly split between developing and industrialised countries. Why are cities in the developing nations growing more rapidly today.
2 Figure 3.3 shows the distribution of urban population in 1990. Using a base map of the world redraw the map showing how you think the situation will change in 2025. Annotate your map explaining your prediction.

FIGURE 3.2 Predicted urban population and mega-city growth

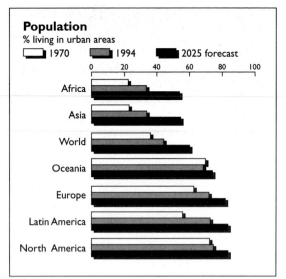

Population
% living in urban areas
☐ 1970 ▨ 1994 ■ 2025 forecast

Africa
Asia
World
Oceania
Europe
Latin America
North America

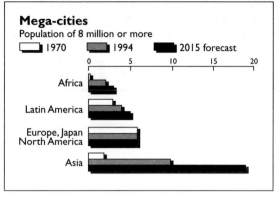

Mega-cities
Population of 8 million or more
☐ 1970 ▨ 1994 ■ 2015 forecast

Africa
Latin America
Europe, Japan North America
Asia

3.3 *Unsustainable cities*

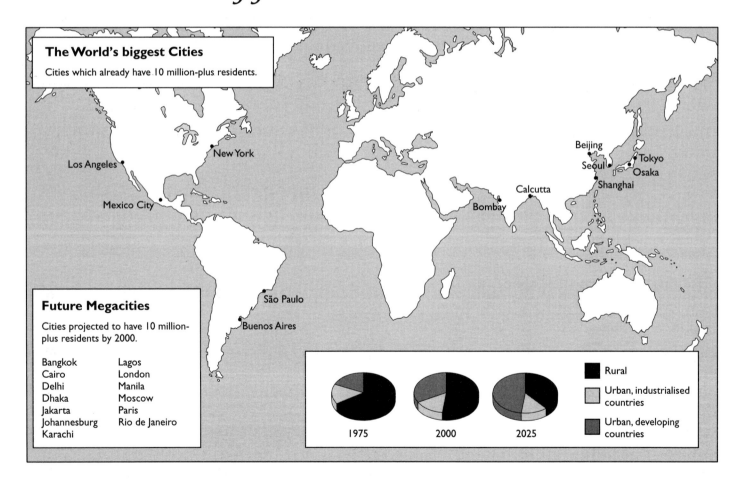

The World's biggest Cities

Cities which already have 10 million-plus residents.

Los Angeles
New York
Mexico City
Beijing
Seoul
Tokyo
Osaka
Shanghai
Calcutta
Bombay
São Paulo
Buenos Aires

Future Megacities

Cities projected to have 10 million-plus residents by 2000.

Bangkok   Lagos
Cairo   London
Delhi   Manila
Dhaka   Moscow
Jakarta   Paris
Johannesburg   Rio de Janeiro
Karachi

■ Rural
☐ Urban, industrialised countries
▨ Urban, developing countries

1975 2000 2025

FIGURE 3.3 The World's biggest cities

Cities are fabricated. They use resources from a periphery which may be local, regional, national or global. They use up resources and create waste which must be disposed of. If we think of cities metabolically, then they ingest vast quantities of energy, water and food. Their activities then produce wastes which include heat, domestic and industrial wastes which must be recycled or removed, and air pollution.

Air pollution is a negative externality. In other

words, it is a problem of which costs are not necessarily borne by those who cause them. Urban atmospheric pollution is caused by the combustion of fossil fuels in our homes, for transport, in electricity production and in industrial processes. It is mainly caused by sulphur dioxide, particulates, lead, nitrogen oxides, carbon monoxide, ozone and the large class of volatile organic compounds. Concentration around the point of discharge may produce levels which can have serious consequences for human, animal and plant health.

FIGURE 3.4 Smog in Mexico City

Student Activity 3.2

Figure 3.5 shows the pollution produced by some of the world's largest cities.

1 Construct an index of pollution for Bangkok, Jakarta, London, Los Angeles, Mexico City, New York, São Paulo and Seoul, where:

- high pollution = 5
- moderate to heavy pollution = 3
- low pollution = 1

To obtain the index, add up each of the scores for the different types of pollution.

2 How true is it to say that urban pollution is a greater problem in the Developing World than in the Developed World? Explain your answer.

Air Pollution in the UK

Figure 3.6 shows that cities like Mexico City have huge problems associated with air pollution. But countries like the UK also suffer from air pollution. A mixture of meterological factors and the rapid rise of car ownership can cause problems. On 5 May 1995 Britain suffered its worst pollution of the year.

FIGURE 3.5 Megadirty mega-cities

	Population (millions) 1990 estimated	2000 projected	Sulphur dioxide	Particulate matter	Lead	Carbon monoxide	Nitrogen dioxide	Ozone
Bangkok	7.16	10.26	○	●	▲	○	○	○
Beijing	9.74	11.47	●	●	○	–	○	▲
Bombay	11.13	15.43	○	●	○	○	○	–
Buenos Aires	11.58	13.05	–	▲	○	–	–	–
Cairo	9.08	11.77	–	●	●	▲	–	–
Calcutta	11.83	15.94	○	●	○	–	○	–
Delhi	8.62	12.77	○	●	○	○	○	–
Jakarta	9.42	13.23	○	●	▲	▲	○	▲
Karachi	7.67	11.57	○	●	●	–	–	–
London	10.57	10.79	○	○	○	▲	○	○
Los Angeles	10.47	10.91	○	▲	○	▲	▲	●
Manila	8.40	11.48	○	●	▲	–	–	–
Mexico City	19.37	24.44	●	●	▲	●	▲	●
Moscow	9.39	10.11	–	▲	○	▲	▲	–
New York	15.65	16.10	○	○	○	▲	○	▲
Rio de Janeiro	11.12	13.00	▲	▲	○	○	–	–
São Paolo	18.42	23.60	○	▲	○	▲	▲	●
Seoul	11.33	12.97	●	●	○	○	○	○
Shanghai	13.30	14.69	▲	●	–	–	–	–
Tokyo	20.52	21.32	○	○	–	○	○	●

● High pollution, ▲ Moderate to heavy pollution, ○ Low pollution, – No data available

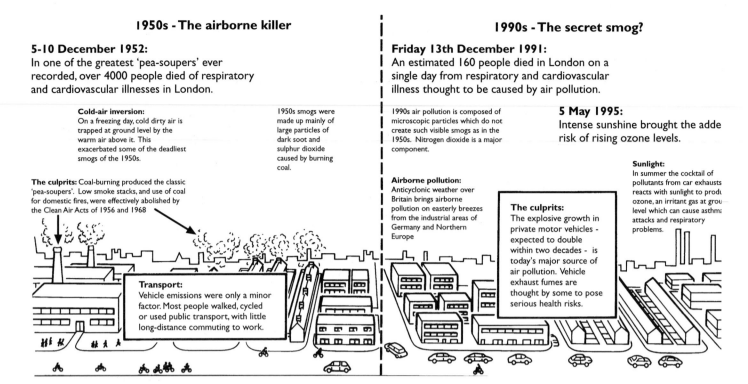

1950s - The airborne killer

5-10 December 1952:
In one of the greatest 'pea-soupers' ever recorded, over 4000 people died of respiratory and cardiovascular illnesses in London.

Cold-air inversion:
On a freezing day, cold dirty air is trapped at ground level by the warm air above it. This exacerbated some of the deadliest smogs of the 1950s.

1950s smogs were made up mainly of large particles of dark soot and sulphur dioxide caused by burning coal.

The culprits: Coal-burning produced the classic 'pea-soupers'. Low smoke stacks, and use of coal for domestic fires, were effectively abolished by the Clean Air Acts of 1956 and 1968

Transport:
Vehicle emissions were only a minor factor. Most people walked, cycled or used public transport, with little long-distance commuting to work.

1990s - The secret smog?

Friday 13th December 1991:
An estimated 160 people died in London on a single day from respiratory and cardiovascular illness thought to be caused by air pollution.

1990s air pollution is composed of microscopic particles which do not create such visible smogs as in the 1950s. Nitrogen dioxide is a major component.

5 May 1995:
Intense sunshine brought the adde risk of rising ozone levels.

Airborne pollution:
Anticyclonic weather over Britain brings airborne pollution on easterly breezes from the industrial areas of Germany and Northern Europe

The culprits:
The explosive growth in private motor vehicles - expected to double within two decades - is today's major source of air pollution. Vehicle exhaust fumes are thought by some to pose serious health risks.

Sunlight:
In summer the cocktail of pollutants from car exhausts reacts with sunlight to prod ozone, an irritant gas at grou level which can cause asthma attacks and respiratory problems.

FIGURE 3.6 Air pollution in London, 1950 and 1990

Still air and strong sunshine combined with pollutants caused discomfort to some people with respiratory illnesses and asthma. There were high ozone levels across the country, with four monitoring stations picking up levels above 90 parts per billion (ppb). The government recommended level is 50 ppb.

3.4 Towards a sustainable City

The future of the world is urban. It is proving impossible to stem the flow of migrants from rural to urban areas. The planned economies of China and Cuba expelled millions from their cities. Indonesia actually outlawed migration but still the metropolitan areas expanded. Rather than stemming the inevitable flow it may be more reasonable to make cities more habitable.

Some experts believe that concentrating the population in urban areas is actually preferable. The argument is that higher densities are less damaging than endless, uncontrolled sprawl. Cities are also very efficient centres from which to disseminate information and administer public welfare:
■ life expectancy is higher in large cities;
■ cities are more likely to have good sewage disposal and running water;
■ they are focuses for medical care, education and jobs.
A sustainable city would have to achieve three things: produce less pollution; use resources more efficiently and retain or improve the standard of living of its residents.

Reducing pollution

Section 3.3 outlined the problems of urban air pollution in cities like Mexico City and London. The villain of the piece is most certainly the motor car. There are half a billion of them now, 19 million more a year, 35 every minute. There are three main ways to counter car culture: technical fixes, physical curbs, and alternative forms of transport. Figure 3.8 outlines some examples of these but also gives reasons why efforts to reduce this pollution have met with only limited success.

Student Activity 3.3

1 In addition to pollution, cars affect the sustainability of cities in the following ways: traffic congestion; urban sprawl; noise.
   a Describe how these factors reduce the sustainability of cities?
   b Choose two of the above and suggest how they could be prevented.
2 What are the advantages over other forms of urban transport.

FIGURE 3.7 Countering the car

Policy	Explanation	Case study	Problems
Technical fix			
■ crisis cars	fuel efficiency rather than speed	Volvo LC P2000 – capable of 100 miles a gallon	oil companies are a powerful lobbying group; must be linked to a carbon tax
■ catalytic converter	removes unburnt hydrocarbons; CO_2, NOx	from 1993 all new cars in the EU must be fitted with CCs	not available in the developing world; must be linked to unleaded fuel
Physical curbs			
■ cut car space	close cities to cars and cut down on parking	Florence has a pedestrianised centre from 7.30am–8.30pm	moves problems somewhere else; 'kills' city centres
■ stop the sprawl	reduce the need for long distance commuting	Toronto is forcing developers to build inner city housing	counterurbanisation is the dominant trend in the west; industries want 'greenfield' sites
■ make drivers pay	the more it costs the less people will drive	in Hong Kong cars are computer logged and made to pay for using the inner city	only effective if linked to good public transport; tends to effect low income group
Other forms of transport			
■ boost the bike	efficient, cheap, quick, clean	Netherlands has 9000 miles of bicycle paths with bike-and-ride schemes	difficult in hilly areas; cyclists find it difficult to co-exist with cars (pollution and danger); poor road surfaces
■ public transport	people will use public transport if it is quick, cheap and realistic	California has introduced an urban light railway; Paris has an underground Metro subsidised by all French tax payers	Effective only if public transport is safe, well funded and subsidised

Transport policy

The traditional geographic concept of 'friction of distance' is becoming less and less important to modern life. The increasing efficiency of modern transport networks of road, rail and air are essential to national development and global integration. The relationship between public and private transport has particular relevance to the sustainability of urban environments. In a society which is increasingly dominated by the car the external costs of congestion, road accidents, pollution, road building, oil burning and loss of habitats are often ignored. Many argue that sustainability can only be achieved by a fundamental change in human behaviour and values.

FIGURE 3.8 Harmonising policies

Government level	Policies
Local	Encourage public transport. Improve traffic management and land use planning.
National	Promote greener modes of travel. Reduce unnecessary travel Make private car ownership more expensive. Instigate a polluter pays policy.
European	Impose community-wide policies on environmental concerns. Ensure a level playing field of fuel costs, vehicle tax and speed limit.

Student Activity 3.4

Figure 3.9 shows how policy solutions can be integrated at a number of levels of government.
1 Suggest actual policies which would meet the requirements stated in Figure 3.9 at:
   a local level
   b national level
   c European level.
2 Why is it necessary to combine policies between these different levels of government?

3.5 Curitiba: A model city

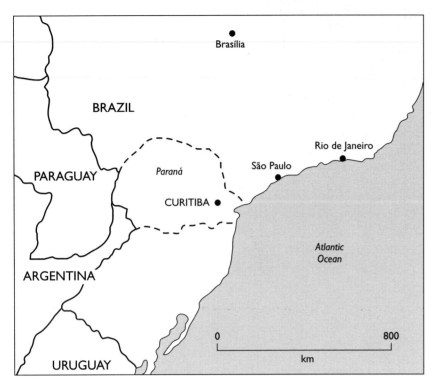

FIGURE 3.9 The location of Curitiba, Brazil

Curitiba is the capital of Paraná state in the south west of Brazil (Figure 3.10). It is held by many to be an excellent model for sustainable urban development. On the surface, Curitiba seems remarkable only in the speed of its population growth. It grew from a modest 300 000 in 1950 to over 2.1 million in 1990. This growth, along with a change from an agricultural to industrial base, should have led to the associated problems of congestion, pollution, under-employment, unsanitary living conditions and squatter settlements if we are to believe the accepted model of Developing World cities. But Curitiba seems to have avoided the worst of these problems.

Planning for the future

Curitiba has developed following a philosophy of urban design very different to the technical fixes used by other cities. Planning proposals have been aligned to a sustainable future in the following ways:
- public transport is preferred over private cars;
- the environment is used rather than changed;
- cheap, low technology solutions are used rather than high technology ones;
- innovation is developed through the participation of citizens (bottom-up) in place of centralised master planning (top-down).

This philosophy was developed by Jaime Lerner – mayor, architect and planner – and has been continued through future administrations. Designing with nature, rather than against it, has meant that flooding is no longer a problem (Figure 3.10). It has also meant that the city has more green space. The amount of parkland has increased from half a square metre per person in 1970 to 50 today.

FIGURE 3.10 Sustainable solutions to flooding

Problems (1950s/60s)	Solutions (late 1960s onwards)
■ many streams had been covered to form underground canals which restricted water flow	■ natural drainage was preserved – these natural flood plains are used as parks
■ houses and other buildings had been built too close to rivers	■ certain low-lying areas are off-limits
■ new buildings were built on poorly drained land on the periphery of the city	■ parks have been extensively planted with trees; existing buildings have been converted into new sports and leisure facilities
■ increase in roads and concrete surfaces accelerated run off	■ bus routes and bicycle paths integrate the parks into the urban life of the city

Linking the city

Most cities grow in a concentric fashion. One zone merges into another zone. Densities increase in the centre whilst the periphery sprawls outwards. Congestion is inevitable as commuters make a diurnal journey between the centre and its surrounds.

The approach to transport in Curitiba is very different. The road network and public transport system have been kept to prescribed structural axes. These allow the city to expand but keep shops, workplaces and homes closely linked.

The main axes

Figure 3.11 shows the five main axes of the three parallel roadways:
- a central road contains two express bus lanes;

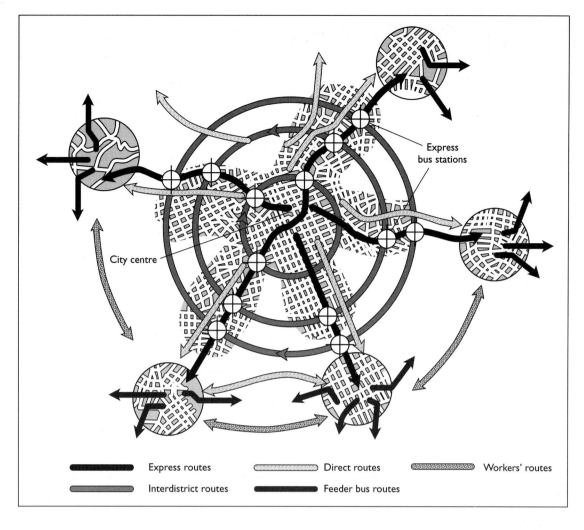

FIGURE 3.11 Curitiba's transit system

Express
bus stations

City centre

Express routes   Direct routes   Workers' routes

Interdistrict routes   Feeder bus routes

FIGURE 3.12 (below) Bus
and stop in Curitiba

■ it is flanked by local roads;
■ one block away to either side run high capacity
one-way streets running into and out of the central
city.
These axes have become the centre of offices and
commerce.

Public transport

Curitiba's mass transit system is based on the bus.
Inter-district and feeder bus routes complement the
express bus lanes along the structural axes.
Everything is geared towards the speed of journey
and convenience of passengers.
■ a single fare allows transfer from express routes
to interdistrict and local buses;
■ extra wide doors allow passengers to crowd on
quickly;
■ double and triple length buses allow for rush
hour loads.
The rationale for the bus system was economy as
well as sustainability. A subway would have cost
$60–$70 million per km – the express bus ways
were only $200 000 per km. The bus companies are
paid by the kilometres of road they serve not the
number of passengers. This ensures that all areas of
the city are served.

Garbage that is not Garbage

Perhaps the biggest lesson from Curitiba is that the problems of a city can be turned into resources. The city's planners also question the idea that every problem should have a high technology fix. An example of both these lessons is the city's 'Garbage that is not Garbage' policy. This involves 70 per cent of households especially in inaccessible low income areas. Poor families can exchange garbage bags for bus tokens, food and school books. Thirty-four thousand families in 62 neighbourhoods have exchanged over 11 000 tonnes of rubbish for nearly a million bus tokens, 1200 tonnes of food, and 1.9 million notebooks.

1 This chapter contains a number of examples of good and bad practice when it comes to sustainable urban growth. Devise your own Green Plan for the sustainable city.

2 Write a sentence on each of the following principles linking them to sustainable urban development:

■ use of appropriate technology, materials and design;
■ redefine indicators of economic and environmental wealth;
■ establish acceptable minimum standards;
■ widespread public participation;
■ ensure that environmental policies are socially equitable;
■ choose the cheapest and simplest solution.

4
SUSTAINABLE WATER

Water is a renewable resource but is also a diminishing resource. ... Demand needs to be managed, or else it may outstrip supply. ... Reductions in average household size, and the increasing trend towards garden watering, have contributed to the increased water consumption by households. Water appliances are, however, becoming more efficient, and industrial water use has fallen. Much public attention has been focused upon the issue of leakage from companies pipes.

(Chairman of OFWAT, 1996)

In the past 'improving' rivers often meant increasing their flow capacity. In future it should refer to multi-purpose schemes designed to improve the capacity of each river valley to function as a visual amenity, a recreation area, a fishery, a nature reserve, a water supply, a storm-detention area, a drainage network area, and a movement corridor for boats, walkers, cyclists and equestrians.

(Tom Turner, Landscape planning, ULC Press Ltd., 1987)

4.1 *The national scene*

By 2050 London's climate will be similar to that of Bordeaux today. The south and east of the UK will become hotter and drier whereas the north and west of the country will become wetter with more frequent flooding. Average UK temperatures will rise from 9°C to 10.6°C, and global sea-levels will rise by about 35 cm. This will cause problems in low lying coastal areas as well as for groundwater in coastal areas. There are a number of implications of these changes:

■ tourism and recreation will increase;
■ farming in upland areas will become more profitable;
■ farming in lowland areas will be subjected to more soil erosion and decreased yields;
■ climatic zones will move northwards by approximately 300 km;
■ increased drought will lead to increased building subsidence;
■ there will be more storms and flooding.

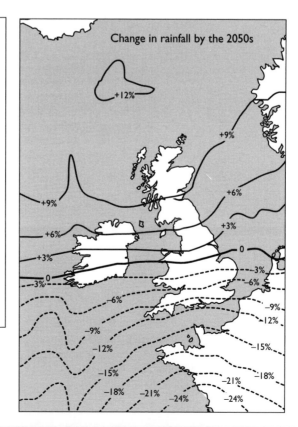

FIGURE 4.1 A wetter north and a drier south

In the UK there is a surplus of water in the north and west of the country and a shortage of water in the south and east, especially in the Thames Region which serves almost a fifth of the nation's population. This pattern is likely to become intensified over the next 20 to 30 years as a result of climatic change (Figure 4.1). It will become increasingly important to maintain a balance between the needs of the water environment, the demands for water and the supply and development of new water resources.

A national strategy for water resource management must include the following issues:
■ sustainable development – there should be no long-term systematic deterioration of the water environment owing to water resources development or water use;
■ precautionary principle – where significant environmental change may occur but understanding of the issues is incomplete, decisions made or measures implemented should err on the side of caution;
■ managing demand – measures should be implemented to minimise losses, for example through better distribution systems and improved efficiency in water use;
■ new schemes – redistribution of water such as the transfer of Severn/Anglian water to the Thames Region.

The Environment Agency (EA) has to manage surface water management, mineral extractions, sewage capacity, water efficiency and demand, waste disposal, habitat enhancement and restoration and research and development. The EA is concerned with the overall policies on water resources, water quality and surface water management, which includes flood defence issues. This is achieved through the licensing of water abstraction, control over discharges and negotiation over granting land drainage consents. The EA has a duty to conserve and enhance the water environment when carrying out any of its functions, and a further duty to promote conservation and enhancement more widely. Increasingly the way to achieve this is through Catchment Management Plans (CMPs).

Research Activity 4.1

For a river of your choice identify opportunities to implement the above criteria. Give specific named examples of each of the five criteria.

4.2 *The role of catchment management plans*

CMPs allow integrated planning of the water environment. They identify appropriate threshold levels for acceptable limits to growth at the location in question (Figure 4.2). CMPs can only be achieved

FIGURE 4.2 Inset guidance for development plans

Where development would cause a risk to water resources, further allocations of land should normally be resisted until adequate resources can be made available.
Current sustainability principles for water resources ensure that:
(i) there should be no long term deterioration of the water environment resulting from water use or water resources for future use;
(ii) reasonable demands for water from both existing and new social and economic development should be satisfied;
(iii) priority should be given to the management of water demand, and to ensure the best use is being made of existing resources. Only if additional water resources are still required will new water resource development be considered;
(iv) in managing water resources, opportunities to enhance the water environment should be identified.
Where new development would be at direct or unacceptable risk from flooding or would aggravate the risk of flooding elsewhere to an unacceptable level proposals should be resisted.

Current sustainability principles for flood defence include:
(i) effective defence for people and property against flooding from rivers and the sea should be provided, together with adequate arrangements for flood forecasting and warning;
(ii) inappropriate development within floodplains should be resisted where such developments would be at risk from flooding or may cause flooding elsewhere;
(iii) flood defence is an intervention in natural processes and therefore a balance has to be struck before maintaining and supporting natural floodplains and alleviating flood risk;
(iv) floodplains should be safeguarded to protect their vital role in allowing for the storage and free-flow of flood waters;
(v) to minimise and increase surface water run-off, new development must be carefully located and designed. Where appropriate, source control measures should be incorporated into the scheme.

through a partnership between a number of key agencies and organisations at a national, regional and local level. CMPs are closely connected with local sustainable development plans, *Agenda 21s* (Figure 4.3).

The key strategic issues with which the Environment Agency will be primarily concerned in the Thames region can be summarised as:
■ the impact of major developments on the water environment and water resources;
■ the impact of major infrastructure proposals on the water environment;
■ the effects of discharges on water quality;
■ the effects of pollution on groundwater;
■ the impact of mineral extraction on the water environment;
■ the impact of waste disposal on the water environment.

Agenda 21 gives a high priority to fresh water, reflecting the management crisis facing the world's freshwater resources. By the year 2000 all countries should have national action programmes for water management, based on catchments, and efficient water-use programmes.

For the EA *Agenda 21* offers:
■ the opportunity to place greater weight on environmental considerations when assessing planning applications;
■ the opportunity to increase community involvement in water uses;
■ help to implement Catchment Management Plans;
■ the opportunity for integration of land-use and water related issues, leading to full-scale integrated catchment management planning;
■ additional opportunities to protect the water environment;
■ increased public awareness of the water environment;
■ help to identify appropriate environmental indicators.

FIGURE 4.3 The water environment and sustainable development

Student Activity 4.2

1 Explain what a catchement management plan is.
2 What is *Agenda 21*?
3 How can rivers be managed in a sustainable way?
4 For a river or river system that you have studied give examples of each of the five principles listed above.

4.3 *Water resources in the Thames Region*

The succession of hot summers in the 1980s and early 1990s heightened the awareness of water resources in the UK. Since the Middle Ages there have only been four droughts that have lasted as long as the recent four year drought of 1989–92. Nevertheless, there should be sufficient water to meet the planned level of growth in most areas across the region in the foreseeable future. However, there remain a number of uncertainties in forecasting demand over the next 20–30 years.

The Thames Region comprises the main drainage basins of the Thames and its tributaries. It is the most densely populated part of the UK, with a population of about 12 million. It covers an area of over 13 000 km² and includes 14 counties, 58 district councils and 33 local planning authorities. The Region comprises the main drainage basin of the River Thames and its tributaries such as the Colne, Lee, Kennet, Wey and Loddon, and covers an area of over 12 900 km². Much of the region, particularly in the west is rural in character, where the dominant land use is agriculture. The River Thames and its tributaries are a vital feature of the physical and human landscape: they are important commercial channels, water supply systems, recreation facilities and support high levels of ecological diversity.

There are considerable development pressures in the region, and these are likely to increase in the future (Figure 4.5). Geologically, the area contains much chalk, limestone, sand and gravel, which creates pressure for mineral extraction. Growth in

FIGURE 4.4 Low rainfall and increased evaporation cause muddy edges to lower lake levels

■ Meeting demand – every day approximately 4700 million litres are abstracted from the region's rivers and groundwater.
■ Alleviation of low flow – of the 20 low flow rivers which are nationally identified as top priority, five are within the Thames Region and another, the River Darent, is closely linked with the London supply system.
■ Managing drought – there is a balance between maintaining environmental requirements, maintaining essential supplies and the imposition of restrictions on certain users. It is impossible to manage for the most severe drought (e.g. a one in a thousand year event) and the worst possible flood (such as Lynmouth in 1952) hence a compromise needs to be reached.
■ Economic development – the region has seen continued growth in housing and commercial development and mineral extraction increasing pressure on land use, water resources and the water environment generally.
■ Water falling in the Cotswolds can be used up to eight times before it reaches the Thames Estuary.

housing and infrastructure creates additional pressures on the water environment and water resources. For example in the Thames Region there is a need for more new housing, the development of derelict sites, mineral extraction, flood defences, a supply of safe drinking water and sustained agricultural yields.

Groundwater resources

The importance of groundwater in the Thames Region cannot be underestimated. There are hundreds of private, domestic and commercial boreholes and springs in daily use. The total volume of groundwater licensed for abstraction amounts to over 2305 million litres per day of which about 85 per cent is used for potable supply. Water companies in the region operate over 300 public supply sources from groundwater. Groundwater also provides a considerable base flow component to many rivers, especially in the upper reaches of the catchment.

Approximately two-thirds of the catchment is permeable and thus subject to direct recharge from rainfall. Polluting discharges may also infiltrate into the ground in these areas. Rainfall varies from 850 mm per year in western parts of the catchment to less than 650 mm per year in the eastern parts. Rates of recharge to groundwater vary considerably from 524 mm per year in the north west to 124 mm per year in the east.

In much of the catchment a situation has been reached where there is no remaining capacity for abstraction because the need to protect streamflows and the valley environment. In some areas over-abstraction has led to reduced flows and the drying

up of some groundwater-fed rivers, particularly on the chalk aquifer. Abstraction in proximity to the Thames estuary has resulted in the transmission of saline waters several kilometres inland (Ghyben-Herzburg principle). A notable exception to the above trend is the chalk aquifer in the London Basin. The considerable reduction in abstractions since 1970 has resulted in rising groundwater levels.

The main groundwater problems have occurred because:
■ flows in several rivers have been depleted as a result of large groundwater abstractions close to the headwaters or along the river valleys. Worst affected are the rivers Misbourne, Wey, Pang and the Letcombe Brook;
■ groundwater has been affected by saline intrusions along the River Thames;
■ most sites which have been considered suitable for waste disposal and landfill are quarries located on aquifers, such as sand and gravel quarried overlying the chalk aquifer, as in south Herts;
■ there is continued pressure for redevelopment of former industrial sites many of which occupy prime locations in urban areas. The land is frequently contaminated and there is often associated groundwater pollution, with possibly considerable pollution potential remaining, especially in areas such as the Thames Gateway;
■ rising nitrate concentrations are evident in other parts of the catchment. In July 1996 the EU criticised the UK for failing to comply with a 1980 Drinking Water Directive. The UK had allowed the level of pesticides in tap water to exceed 0.1 mg/L. Certain parts of the country, especially London and the South East, were affected;
■ groundwater in some urban areas has been contaminated by leakage from sewers and through widespread usage of chemicals such as solvents;
■ the EU Groundwater Action Programme aims to improve the integration of water planning into agricultural, industrial and regional planning. Over-exploitation and pollution are widespread. Member states are expected to prepare national programmes to identify, map and protect groundwater resources by the year 2000. In the EU just over 65 per cent of drinking water supplies come from groundwater. Between 1970 and 1985 demand increased by 35 per cent.

Trends in water use

The vast majority of water abstracted in the Region is for drinking water supply. Almost 60 per cent of the water for public supplies comes from surface water supplies, mainly from the Thames and the Lee in association with the major surface reservoirs around London. On average 150 litres are used per person per day in the home, the majority of which is used to flush toilets, take baths and showers and use the washing machine.

Water use in the home accounts for 45 per cent of the total public water supply demand. A further 27 per cent of the public water supply is used by industry and commerce. The remaining 28 per cent across the region is lost through leakage from distribution and trunk mains systems, and supply pipes on customer premises.

Over the last 20 years demand for public water supplies has increased by approximately 1.7 per cent each year. The key factors which have influenced demand are:
■ the use of water in the home and garden;
■ losses through leakage from distribution systems and consumers' plumbing;
■ population growth and household size;
■ development pressure and economic activity.
The trend in growth of demand has been significantly reduced in recent years owing to improvements by water companies in controlling losses, a decline in economic activity within the region and increased awareness and publicity over drought related issues (Figure 4.7).

FIGURE 4.6 (above) Integrated water management at Farmoor reservoir water storage and recreation

The main areas of uncertainty regarding water demand and supply are:
■ land use planning;
■ resilience of water supply system;
■ climatic change;
■ environmental acceptability of any new water resource scheme:
■ changing patterns of development;
■ uptake of household appliances and levels of ownership;
■ gardening habits;
■ population growth and household size;
■ levels of economic activity;
■ the methods of charging for water and the price level adopted;
■ the effectiveness of demand management measures, particularly control of losses through leakage;
■ agricultural change.

Managing future demands

Managing the growth in demand will require a combination of methods such as leakage control, selective metering and improvements in water efficiency. Many water efficient appliances are now available such as low water-use washing machines, low flush toilet cisterns and water-wise gardening products. There is also likely to be a change in the demand for water. Demand for manufacturing industry is likely to decline since the patterns of manufacturing are changing and companies are becoming more efficient at using water. Future agricultural demands depend mainly on changes in agricultural policy. The growth in tourism and recreation will increase the demand for water. For example, the restoration of disused canals may become a pressure on water resources. There are a number of restoration projects currently being considered in the region.

Recent experience of the promotion of major new water resource schemes indicates that it can take between 15 and 20 years from starting feasibility studies to commissioning a new scheme. The planning of schemes required by the year 2017 should begin in 1997.

FIGURE 4.7 (left) Factors affecting water demand

Student Activity 4.3

1 State two reasons why rainfall is higher in the West Thames Region than in the East.
2 Give two reasons why evapotranspiration rates are higher in the East than in the West.
3 What is groundwater? Explain why groundwater reserves are declining in the Thames area.
4 Explain why demand for water is increasing in the Thames Region.

Water resource development options in the Thames Region

A number of options have been considered but rejected (Figure 4.8), at least for the present, on financial and/or environmental costs. These include:
■ use of gravel workings for storage;
■ redevelopment of existing resources;
■ freshwater storage in the tidal Thames Estuary;
■ inter-regional transfers from Wales via the River Wye, Northumbria (Kielder Water) and Scotland;
■ desalination of water.

FIGURE 4.8 (right)
Warmer summers mean
more water is used in
gardens

Options which are carried forward for further
evaluation include:
■ London basin groundwater including artificial
recharge;
■ (riverside) groundwater development
opportunities;
■ re-allocation of under-utilised resources;
■ re-use of effluents presently discharged into the
tidal Thames Estuary;
■ reservoir storage in south west Oxfordshire;
■ inter-regional transfer from the River Severn and
the Anglian Region.

FIGURE 4.9 Resource
Development options

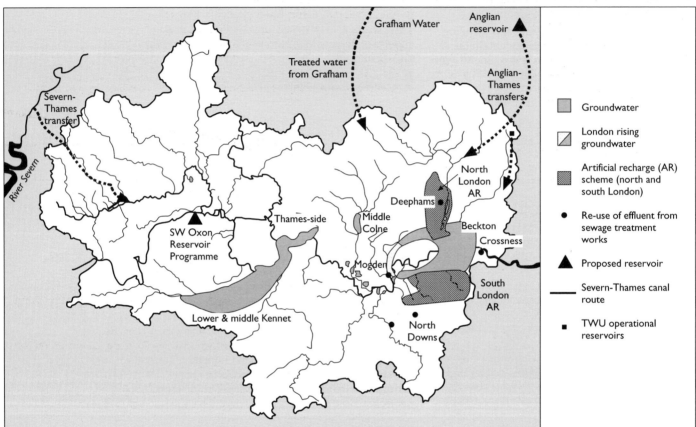

DME

DECISION MAKING EXERCISE 4.4

■ For each of the four options outline its potential
advantages and disadvantages.
■ Which scheme is a) the cheapest b) most
expensive?
■ Which has most long term potential?
■ What are the environmental effects of each
scheme?
■ Write a 200-word letter in support of one scheme.
■ Write a 200-word letter against any one scheme.
Using as much evidence as possible, outline a case
for the development of water resources in the
Thames Region. You may choose up to three of the
options mentioned above to form an integrated
approach to sustainable development. You must
reject at least one of the options.

*Key selected information on some of the remaining
options*

1 London Basin groundwater
The confined chalk aquifer of the London Basin
provides an extensive natural storage body which
has very limited connection with the river systems.
During the early part of the century, water levels in
the aquifer in North and Central London fell owing
to over-abstraction leaving a large volume of empty
aquifer. Since the 1940s abstractions have decreased
so that in most parts of London, especially the
central area, water levels are now rising. Artificial
recharge during times of surplus, largely in winter,
are almost complete in North London and a similar
scheme is being investigated for South and Central
London. Rising groundwater levels may pose a
threat to foundations and tunnels constructed while
levels were depressed.

2 Transfers from the River Severn and Anglian water

This would involve transferring and mixing water from the River Severn into the River Thames. It would secure supplies of water during periods of naturally low flows. However there are the infrastructure and water treatment implications, costs and feasibility of an inter-basin transfer of different river water qualities.

There are also environmental implications due to the potential need for additional reservoir storage in Wales, and regulation of the River Severn. Development in conjunction with the restoration of the Thames and Severn canal has been ruled out on engineering feasibility and cost grounds.

3 A new reservoir

The NRA proposed a new reservoir for South West Oxfordshire. The plan was for the reservoir to store water from the Thames during high flows, supply the Upper Thames area and supply the Thames during low flow. However, changes in demand and the more efficient conservation of water have meant that the project has been deferred, at least for the present. There are a number of issues that need to be considered.

(i) On-site
- pollution risks during construction
- effect of the reservoir on flood risk and drainage
- diversion of water courses
- effect on groundwater levels (leakage from reservoir)

(ii) Operational effects
- the physical, chemical and ecological implications of abstraction from the Thames
- maintaining reservoir water quality in terms of oxygen, algal and temperature characteristics (effects of these on return to the Thames in low flow

(iii) Benefits
- security of water resources
- restoration of the Wilts–Berks canal

FIGURE 4.10 Discarded options for water resource development in the Thames region

Option	Yield	Cost	Environmental Impact	Reasons for rejection
Freshwater storage in the tidal Thames estuary, i.e. Thames Barrier as a barrage	up to 200 Ml/d	MOD– HIGH	HIGH	■ rise in groundwater levels could effect stability of buildings and underground services; ■ restrictions to navigation through barriers; ■ changes in siltation patterns; ■ increase in flooding risks; ■ significant ecological impacts, e.g. Syon Park SSSI; ■ pollution risk from sewage treatment works and storm outfalls; ■ change in tidal character of the river; ■ significant legal implications, i.e. amendment of Barrier Act required to allow change of use
Transfer from River Wye to Upper Thames – transfers supported by regulating storage; – run of river transfer from Lower Wye without further flow augmentation	–	MOD	MOD–HIGH	■ reservoir in Wye valley only required to supply the Thames Region; ■ unreliable without regulating storage. River Wye low flows are not well maintained; ■ engineering feasibility in question; ■ longer periods when transfer unavailable; ■ smaller transfer volume than Severn–Thames transfer; ■ longer, more costly transfer route with greater environmental impact
Imports from Northumbria (Kielder Reservoir) by river/aqueduct	?	HIGH	LOW	■ high transmission costs; ■ high capital and operating costs – uncompetitive compared to river to river transfers
Kielder–London submarine pipeline	200 Ml/d	HIGH	LOW–MOD	■ cost makes it only viable in absence of the regional options; ■ not yet fully investigated
Imports from Northumbria/Scotland by sea – towing storage tanks behind ocean going tugs	100–200? Ml/d	HIGH	LOW	■ more expensive compared to other resource options with few compensating advantages
Redevelopment of existing reservoirs	70–150 Ml/d	HIGH	HIGH	■ would require a major new resource substitute during redevelopment; ■ temporary loss of SSSI; ■ significant local disturbance
Desalination	?	HIGH	HIGH	■ consistent source water quality required and low pollution risk; ■ land availability dictates sites away from Thames estuary; ■ energy intensive; ■ abstraction of seawater and discharge of brine could create significant environmental impacts; ■ to produce potable quality water requires blending and chemical dosing, increasing production costs; ■ high transmission, operation, power and production costs make the option uncompetitive

Option	Yield (Ml/d)	Indicative capital expenditure (£ million)
London Basin Groundwater:		
North London Artificial Recharge	90	11
South London Artificial Recharge	90	16
Rising Groundwater	30	*
Other Groundwater:		
Thames-side	50	1
Lower and Middle Kennet	20–50	4
North Downs	5	*
Lower Greensand	*	*
Effluent Re-use	100	25
South-West Oxfordshire Reservoir Proposal	350	450
Severn–Thames Transfer:		
to Buscot (200 Ml/d)	120	52
to SW Oxfordshire Reservoir (200 Ml/d)	145	62
to London (pipeline)	200?	160
Anglian–Thames Transfer:		
via River Thame (with storage)		190
via Grafham	up to	150
via Stort	100	125
via Roding		125

FIGURE 4.11 Costs of the various options for water resource development

4 Re-use of water

A number of possibilities exist:
- recycling by industry and power generation;
- possible 'grey-water' uses (water which may be recycled or treated to a lower level than drinking water). For example, use for flushing toilets or outside uses (car washes, gardens, sports grounds and irrigation);
- the use of high grade treated effluent to supplement existing water resources available to London which would otherwise be discharged to tidal waters.

The feasibility of further re-use depends upon a number of factors, principally the achievement standards to meet drinking water and public health requirements, and the provision of adequate environmental protection to rivers.

FIGURE 4.12 Environmental impacts of each option

The table below records environmental impacts for each engineering option across four groups — **Sensitivity to change**, **Potential environmental risks (Construction)**, **Potential environmental risks (Operation)** and **Environmental opportunities** — each assessed against eight criteria: Aquatic Ecology, Terrestrial Ecology, Water Quality, Recreation and Navigation, Agriculture, Community Impacts, Archaeology and Heritage, and Planning and General Landscape including Built Environment. Impact magnitude is shown as Low (•), Medium (●) or High (⬤); a diagonal stroke (/) indicates that the impact can be mitigated.

Engineering options	Sensitivity to change	Construction	Operation	Environmental opportunities
LONDON BASIN GROUNDWATER	Terrestrial •	Archaeology •	Water Quality •	Aquatic •, Terrestrial •, Landscape •
North London Artificial Recharge	Terrestrial •	Aquatic /, Terrestrial /, Water Quality •	Water Quality •	Aquatic •, Terrestrial •, Landscape •
South London Artificial Recharge	Terrestrial •		Water Quality •	
Rising groundwater				
OTHER GROUNDWATER				
Thames-side Groundwater	Aquatic •, Terrestrial •, Recreation •, Agriculture •	Aquatic •, Terrestrial •, Agriculture •, Community •	Water Quality •, Archaeology •	
Lower & Middle Kennet	Aquatic •, Terrestrial •, Recreation •, Agriculture •	Aquatic •, Terrestrial •	Water Quality •	
North Downs	Aquatic •, Terrestrial •	Aquatic •, Terrestrial •	Water Quality •	Aquatic •, Terrestrial •
Lower Greensand	Aquatic •, Terrestrial •, Water Quality •	Aquatic •, Terrestrial •, Agriculture •	Water Quality •	Aquatic •, Terrestrial •
OPPORTUNITIES FOR REALLOCATION	Aquatic •			Aquatic •, Terrestrial •, Recreation •, Community •
EFFLUENT REUSE	Aquatic •, Terrestrial •, Water Quality ●, Recreation •	Community •	Aquatic •, Terrestrial •, Water Quality •, Community •	
SW OXFORDSHIRE RESERVOIR PROPOSAL (SWORP)				
On-site	Aquatic ⬤, Terrestrial ⬤, Water Quality ●, Recreation •, Agriculture ⬤, Community •, Archaeology •	Aquatic ⬤/, Terrestrial ●/, Water Quality ⬤/, Recreation •, Agriculture •, Community ⬤, Archaeology ⬤, Landscape ⬤	Aquatic /, Terrestrial /, Water Quality ⬤, Recreation •, Agriculture •, Community ⬤, Archaeology •, Landscape ⬤	Aquatic /, Terrestrial ⬤, Water Quality ⬤, Recreation ●, Agriculture ⬤, Community •, Landscape ⬤
River Thames & River Corridor	Aquatic ⬤, Terrestrial ●, Water Quality ⬤, Recreation ●, Agriculture •	Aquatic ⬤/, Terrestrial ⬤/, Water Quality ⬤/, Recreation •	Aquatic ⬤/, Terrestrial ⬤/, Water Quality ⬤, Recreation •	Aquatic ⬤, Terrestrial ●, Water Quality ●, Recreation •, Agriculture •, Landscape ⬤
SEVERN–THAMES TRANSFER				
to Buscot	Aquatic ⬤, Terrestrial ⬤, Water Quality ⬤, Recreation •, Agriculture •, Community •, Archaeology •, Landscape •	Aquatic ⬤/, Terrestrial ⬤/, Water Quality ⬤/, Recreation /, Agriculture •, Community •, Landscape •	Water Quality •, Community •, Archaeology •, Landscape •	Aquatic •, Terrestrial •, Archaeology •, Landscape •
to SWORP (pipeline)	Aquatic •, Terrestrial •, Water Quality •, Community •, Landscape •	Aquatic •, Terrestrial •, Agriculture •	Water Quality •	
to London (pipeline)	Aquatic •	Water Quality •, Community •	Water Quality •	
ANGLIAN–THAMES TRANSFER				
via Grafham	Aquatic •	Recreation •, Community •, Archaeology •		
Via Rivers: Thame, Sort and Roding	Aquatic ⬤, Terrestrial ⬤, Water Quality •, Recreation •, Agriculture •, Community •	Aquatic •, Terrestrial ⬤, Water Quality •, Recreation •, Agriculture •, Community ⬤	Aquatic •, Terrestrial ●, Water Quality ⬤, Recreation •, Agriculture •, Community •, Archaeology •	

Key

Aquatic Ecology

Terrestrial Ecology

Water Quality

Recreation and Navigation

Agriculture

Community Impacts

Archaeology and Heritage

Planning and General Landscape including Built Environment

• Low ● Medium ⬤ High / Impact can be Mitigated

5
OPTIONS FOR SUSTAINABLE AGRICULTURE IN DEVELOPING COUNTRIES

5.1 Introduction

Rural areas are especially important in LEDCs. They account for a large proportion of the work force as well as providing food and export earnings. For about one-fifth of the population of LEDCs environmental concerns and development needs are focused upon immediate survival and are local and rurally based (Elliot, 1994). Change is ever present. Food productivity in many areas is falling, and environmental quality is deteriorating as inappropriate development exceeds the land's capacity to cope. Nearly three-quarters of the world's drylands are degraded, and desertification costs an estimated $42 million annually. The amount of farmland per person has fallen from 0.38 ha per head in 1970 to 0.28 ha per head in 1990 and is estimated to fall to 0.15 by the year 2050. There have been many schemes to increase agricultural productivity in LEDCs, notably the Green Revolution. However, this has not always succeeded and critics claim that it is causing great damage to the physical and social environment. Irrigation schemes have also had adverse effects. So are there any possibilities of developing sustainable agriculture in LEDCs?

This chapter presents material from a semi-arid area of South Africa, the former homeland of Ciskei, arguably one of the most degraded rural areas in the developing world. Ciskei is a 'resource poor' marginal agricultural area. The majority of farmers have limited access to resources and technology. However there are examples of sustainable agricultural development, especially those which are small-scale, locally based and usually organised by women and non-government organisations (NGOs) such as Operation Hunger in South Africa.

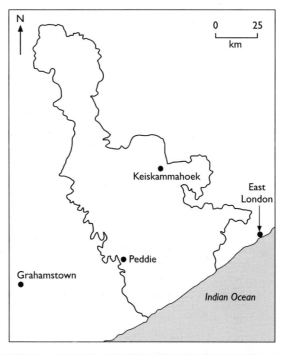

FIGURE 5.1 The location of the former homeland of Ciskei

5.2 A case study of sustainable agriculture in Ciskei

Physical background

The former Ciskei homeland covered a small area, less than 8000 km², on the southern coast of South Africa. With a population of approximately 1 million people it was described as one of South Africa's largest rural slums. The area comprises four major sub-divisions: the coast belt, the dissected coastal plateau, the Amatola Basin and the semi-arid mountainous Hewu district in the north. Only the Amatola Basin has much potential for agriculture: the rest is characterised by a mixture of poor soils, steep slopes, low and irregular rainfall and a short growing season.

The region experiences mostly summer convectional rainfall, with more than 70 per cent of the rain occurring between October and November. Coastal areas have a more even distribution. By contrast, rainfall is lowest and most irregular in the northern district. Drought in the late 1970s, 1980s and early 1990s reduced agricultural potential even further. Temperature ranges are greatest in the north of the region and the incidence of frost also limits the growing season. Soils are generally unsuitable for rain-fed cultivation, although there are a few areas with good potential soils. Most of the area comprises valley bushveld which is poor for grazing but suitable for browsing. Only a tenth is good for grazing.

FIGURE 5.2 Climatic data for Ciskei

Political and Economic factors

The Ciskei developed as one of the homelands under the apartheid system. In the early twentieth century a number of Reserve Lands existed for sole African occupation, but it was not until 1913 that the South African government attempted to impose order on a chaotic land situation. The 1913 Native Land Act provided land for Africans to own and occupy. The reserves had two functions: to provide a steady supply of cheap labour for the mines and to segregate blacks from whites. The 1936 Native Trust and Land Act, added a further 6.2m ha to the amount set aside earlier. However, population growth over the following decades led to increasing population pressure, not to agricultural innovation or intensification as it had earlier or elsewhere. Soil erosion, soil exhaustion, emigration and poverty became endemic in the homelands. The rural areas increasingly ceased to look to agriculture as their main source of subsistence and many of the younger males became migrant labourers, working on the mines in the Transvaal, thereby depriving the homelands of their greatest resource, their labourers. Despite eventual 'independence', less than 20 per cent of the homeland populations derived their income from the geographical area of their 'homelands'. Ciskei, for example, derived only between 10 and 17 per cent of its income from within Ciskei territory.

A profile of agriculture in Ciskei

In general the Ciskei is an area of arable agriculture rather than pastoral farming. Most cultivation is of a subsistence nature. Agricultural productivity is low and variable for a number of reasons. Physical factors include low and irregular rainfall, poor soils, limited vegetation quality and steep slopes. Output is also affected by access to the land, which is determined by the tenure system, sharing and rental agreements. Other constraints include the high cost of seeds, water and the lack of fences to deter domestic animals. Theft and the high risk of operations further reduced the incentive to farm the land. Shortage of labour is also a problem. The large number of female headed households and absent males is characteristic of areas of low productivity. In some cases the absence of males caused some households to abandon agriculture altogether. The agricultural potential has been so eroded that most rural people rely on migrant remittances for their livelihood. Indeed, earnings from agriculture account for less than 10 per cent of household income for the majority of rural households. Although livestock holdings are one of the best indicators of capital accumulation, in Ciskei this is generally not the case since there are better alternatives to agriculture. Essentially the inability of the land to provide a sufficient supply of food

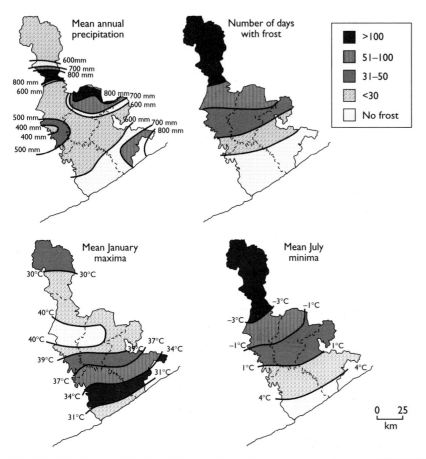

Mean annual precipitation

600mm
700 mm
800 mm
800 mm
600 mm
800 mm 700 mm
600 mm
500 mm
400 mm
400 mm
500 mm
500 mm
600 mm 700 mm
800 mm

Number of days with frost

■	>100
▨	51–100
▨	31–50
░	<30
□	No frost

Mean January maxima

30°C 30°C
40°C
40°C 37°C
39°C 34°C
37°C 31°C
34°C
31°C

Mean July minima

–3°C –1°C
–3°C
–1°C 1°C
1°C 4°C
4°C

0   25
km

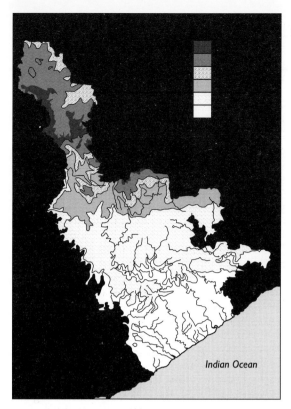

Sustainable options: small-scale gardens and subsistence farms

The promotion of small vegetable gardens and subsistence farms is urged, as they could provide a very useful extra supply of food. Indeed, returns from vegetable gardens can be made after only six weeks, especially with carrots. Groundnuts, spinach and beans are foods which also grow well in the area and provide a valuable source of protein which could be used to enrich the staples. If such gardens are integrated with improvements in harvesting and storage there ought to be a much larger supply of quality food at very little cost.

To overcome the problem of local economic and political poverty, farming cooperatives consisting mostly of women could be developed. There is a pool of labour and experience, the latter perhaps somewhat limited, which could share the cost of tools and seed, and use the produce for their subsistence needs.

Theft in all areas remains a problem, as does the trampling of crops by livestock. This could, in part, be reduced by the erection of fences or barbed wire, a task which could become a cottage industry in itself. Water supplies would also need to be extended in order to provide sufficient quantity for crop growth, and animal dung could be collected on a more regular basis and used as fertiliser. As well as the impact on farm yields and food storage, these schemes offer good prospects for local economic development, a 'bottom-up' approach which will provide a small amount of employment for local people.

FIGURE 5.3 Relief in Ciskei

and a regular, reliable source of income meant that farming in Ciskei was inefficient and marginal. Paradoxically, although the land is unable to support the population much of the land remains unutilised. Subsistence farmers have often been targeted by planners so as to increase their yields from vegetable gardens. However, the cost of starting a vegetable garden is frequently beyond the means of the people.

Student Activity 5.1

1 Why should theft be such a problem in the former Ciskei?
2 Why is there a shortage of labour? Give contrasting reasons to suggest why such a high proportion of the land should be left unused.
3 Explain why female headed households should be associated with low levels of agricultural productivity. What are the development implications of gender?

Increasing agricultural productivity

There are many possibilities of improving agricultural productivity in the region. On the one hand there are expensive irrigation schemes such as at Keiskammahoek and at the agricultural research centre at Fort Hare. On the other, there are less expensive, less glamorous schemes such as the promotion of vegetable gardens, and dryland techniques and crops that can tolerate water scarcity. This section examines some of the alternatives and considers developments on two scales: small-scale gardens and larger-scale commercial and subsistence farming.

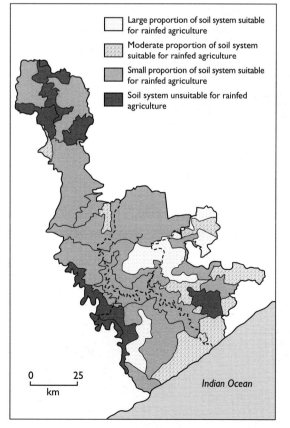

FIGURE 5.4 Soil types in Ciskei

Large proportion of soil system suitable for rainfed agriculture

Moderate proportion of soil system suitable for rainfed agriculture

Small proportion of soil system suitable for rainfed agriculture

Soil system unsuitable for rainfed agriculture

0   25
km

Indian Ocean

The increased use of goats and sheep could provide a valuable supply of milk and wool. This may produce an important cash income for many of the poorer households. Herds need to be tended better than at the present, since many large herds can regularly be seen on the roadside. Indeed, if there was more control over these flocks, their usefulness would be improved. Nevertheless, the large amount of scrubland that is unused at present represents a resource wasted. This could provide valuable fodder, which in turn could be converted into milk, meat and money.

There is the danger that the promotion of cash crops could have poor nutritional consequences and might lead to a breakdown in traditional sharing practices. The sale of nutritive legumes may mean that the household diet suffers in terms of quality of food as fresh food would be replaced with bought food. Production of cash crops may make sense economically but not necessarily nutritionally. Over-dependence on cash crops may also increase the risk of failure in bad years. On the other hand, much of Ciskei is semi-arid and is of poor potential for nutritional crops and so could be used for the development of certain oils and perfumes or drought resistant crops such as saltbrush.

Any redistribution of land into workable units will necessitate the extension, or in some places creation, of a class of rural landless people. Increased migration to metropolitan areas may reduce the number, but many will need to be accommodated by some form of small-scale labour intensive rural employment scheme, such as road construction, dam building or food storage

schemes, on a long term basis. Developments in agricultural technology may also reduce the numbers employed on the land and thus it is imperative to create other forms of employment in rural areas.

Other possibilities include long-term state-sponsored initiatives. Incomes could be raised in a number of ways: labour intensive agriculture; increased social welfare payments; industries to create employment, including small-scale projects such as gardens, food-storage schemes, water-storage and purification plants.

Small-holder irrigation in Ciskei

Irrigation is playing an increasingly important role in order to combat decreasing levels of food per head throughout many African countries. However, irrigation is relatively insignificant in African agriculture: of a total of 150 million ha of cultivated land in Africa only 9 per cent is irrigated, 75 per cent of which is in Egypt, Sudan and Madagascar. Moreover little is known about the performance of schemes, especially in terms of social, economic and institutional impact.

The Tyefu irrigation scheme was established in 1976 in one of the most eroded, impoverished and drought stricken areas of Ciskei. After negotiations with the Tyefu Tribal Authority, the land was divided into:
a commercial estate of 103 ha;
a commercial 'tribal farm' of 194 ha designed to provide a comprehensive range of services to farmers, and to use profits for local community development;

FIGURE 5.5 Tyefu, Ciskei

224 plots of 0.25 ha for all those with land rights, subsistence and small surplus;
30 commercial farms of 4 ha for locals who wish to go into full-time agriculture.
The results were:
- 220 full-time jobs; 1210 part-time jobs;
- surrounding areas benefited by buying surplus maize;
- multiplier effect (ancillary industries and provision of services);
- operating costs exceeded returns (operating costs will decrease over time);
- individual incomes for farmers were not as good as urban incomes: more incentives were needed for farmers.

Relatively successful irrigation projects such as Gezira in Sudan and Mwea in Kenya, and failures such as Rachad in Sudan, Kano in Nigeria and Qamata in South Africa suggest that success depends on the integration of management, participants, the socio-economic conditions and technology availability.

The causes of failure are complex. They include a mixture of technicality, financing, management and criteria for success. For example, greater yields and higher incomes do not necessarily mean success if there is increased indebtedness, rural landless, and very high rents or subsidies to produce the food.

The pre-requisites for successful small holder irrigation include:
- political commitment on national and local levels;
- economic assessments must take into account the 'unquantifiable', such as the effect on social systems, risks;
- irrigation must be linked to commercial agriculture;
- land tenure changes need to be sorted out first;
- extension services (education, credit, marketing, storage) must be provided;
- farmer participation should be involved in the project at a very early stage.

The establishment of drought resistant fodder crops

Pastureland in the Ciskei is especially fragile owing to a combination of drought, overgrazing, population pressure and the absence of land ownership policies. During prolonged drought, levels of cattle, sheep and goats decrease significantly. However, trying to decrease herd size has proved unpopular and unsuccessful. An alternative is to produce drought resistant fodder crops, e.g. American Aloe (*Agave Americana*) and the prickly pear (*opunta. sp.*), saltbrush and the indigenous Gwanish (*spekboom*).

The American Aloe has traditionally been used for fencing, for kraals (animal compounds) and for soil conservation, but has been used as a fodder in times of drought. It has a number of advantages:
- it requires little moisture;
- it is not attacked by any insects;
- although low in protein, it raises milk production in cows;
- it can be used for soil conservation;
- after 10 years it produces a pole that can be used for fencing or building;

FIGURE 5.6 Aloe plants

- it can act as a wind break;
- the juice of the aloe is used in the production of tequila.

Salt brush provides protein rich fodder which is eaten by sheep and goats. Goats, in particular, thrive on salt brush. It requires less than half of the water that other crops, such as Lucerne require, and once established requires no irrigation. It remains green throughout the year and therefore can provide all year fodder. However, it is difficult to propagate and needs high quality management.

The spineless cactus or prickly pear features prominently in the agriculture of many LEDCs such as Mexico, Tunisia, and Peru where they are used as a fodder crop and as a fruit crop for 2–3 months each year. They are becoming more widespread in Ciskei. Two varieties are common – one, insect-resistant, is used as fodder in times of drought, while the other, which needs to be sprayed to reduce insect damage, yields high quality fruit. The fruit is sold at prices comparable with apples and oranges. Pruning is needed annually. This provides up to 100 tonnes of fodder per hectare per year.

As a result of drought in the 1980s the Ciskei government embarked on a series of trials with prickly pear, saltbrush and American Aloe in order to create more fodder. One of the main advantages of the prickly pear is its low water requirements. This makes it very suitable to the Ciskei area where rainfall is low and unreliable. Although there are intensive irrigation schemes in the region, such as at Keiskammahoek, these are expensive and inappropriate to the area and the people.

Although prickly pear is mainly used as a fodder and fruit crop, it is also used for the production of carminic acid for the cochineal dye industry and as a means of soil conservation. Nevertheless, prickly pear has been described by some development planners as 'a weed, the plant of the poor, a flag of misery, ... inconsistent with progress'.

Essential oils

The production of essential oils holds considerable potential as a form of sustainable agricultural development in the Ciskei. Not only are the raw materials present but it is a labour intensive industry and would utilise a large supply of unemployed and underemployed people.

The essential oils industry has a number of advantages:
- it is a new or additional source of income for many people;
- it is labour intensive and local in nature;
- many plants are already known and used by the people as medicines, and are therefore culturally acceptable;
- in their natural state the plants are not very palatable nor of great value and will not therefore be stolen;
- many species are looked on as weeds. Removing these regularly improves grazing potential as well as supplying raw materials for the essential oils industry.

FIGURE 5.7 Prickly pear plants

Some species such as Geranium, peppermint and sage require too much land, labour and water to be very successful. Wild als (*artemisia afra*) is an indigenous mountainous shrub, used for the treatment of colds. Its oil has a strong medicinal fragrance, and is used in deodorants and soaps. Double cropping in summer when the plant is still growing and in autumn at the end of the growing season yields the best results. Demand for *artemisia* has now outstripped the supply of wild material. It is increasingly cultivated as a second crop. It requires minimal input in terms of planting, village, pest control etc. and is relatively easy to establish and manage. Moreover, it can stabilise many of the maize fields and slopes where soil erosion is now a problem. The local population are very enthusiastic especially given the right economic incentives.

Khakibush (*Tagetes minuta*) is an annual aromatic. In Ciskei it is the most common weed in most maize fields. Oil of Tagetes is an established essential oil, although its market is limited. Local people are again quite enthusiastic about collecting khakibush if the incentives are there. Harvesting takes up to three months and provides a great deal of extra employment, as well as eradicating a weed. At present the use of wild Tagetes and those in the maize fields is sufficient to meet demand. An increase in demand might lead to the establishment of Tagetes as a secondary crop in maize fields – not just as a 'weed'.

Rabbit production

Rabbit production is a useful additional source of agricultural production for a number of reasons:
- space requirements are low;
- they are a valuable food source, high in protein, low in cholesterol;
- they can bring in extra income;
- they are very productive (32 day gestation, 150 day generation gap);
- they do not compete with humans for food but can use kitchen and garden waste, weeds, leaves of trees and shrubs;
- they have low starting costs;
- rabbit dung can be used as fertiliser;
- work can be done by women and children.
   However, there are a number of considerations:
- rabbits are totally dependent upon man for feeding and care;
- they require more attention than range animals;
- rabbit production is relatively underdeveloped in Ciskei therefore much education and extension services are required;
- it is labour intensive;
- an initial investment is needed for housing;
- there are problems of predators;
- in drier areas, supplementary feeding may be needed;
- rabbits are not native to South Africa.

FIGURE 5.8 Small scale vegetable farming at a school in Ndevana

The typical diet in the region consists of a cereal-based main meal, a maize-based porridge, normally supplemented with vegetables and fruit. Meat intake in rural areas is relatively low. Milk is often the main source of protein. Hence rabbits are a potential source of much needed animal protein.

Many households consist of women and children only. Many males are absent at work and in many households there is no man. Female-headed households are particularly marginal – the women must support the household financially as well as in other ways. There is limited scope for labour intensive agriculture. However, a rabbit hutch kept close to the house could be tended by children. Rabbit units could also be established alongside school vegetable gardens or community gardens, where fodder is available and the dung can be used as fertiliser.

Student Activity 5.2

1 Evaluate the schemes outlined above for Ciskei in terms of their
  (i)   social and cultural acceptability,
  (ii) environmental sustainability,
  (iii) economic and technical appropriateness and
  (iv) local political manageability.
2 Which forms of sustainable agriculture are best for Ciskei? Why?
3 The Green Revolution has been described as the application of science to increase agricultural yields. Describe and explain the geographic consequences of the Green Revolution in a country or area that you have studied. How far do you agree that the Green Revolution is a form of sustainable development? Give reasons for your answer.
4 For any region that you have studied in an LEDC, assess how useful any of the above schemes may be as a means of increasing agricultural productivity. Explain your answer in detail.

6
SUSTAINABLE TOURISM

6.1 Introduction

The tourist industry is now one of the world's largest industries. The number of foreign holidays rose from approximately 25 million in 1950 to over 350 million in the mid-1990s. Annual revenue from tourism of over $300 billion, represents 5.5 per cent of world GNP.

The rise in tourism is related to a number of economic and social trends:

- increased leisure time;
- cheaper, faster forms of transport;
- an increase in disposable income;
- the growth of the package holiday;
- greater media exposure, travel programmes etc.;
- a rise in the number of second holidays, short breaks etc.

The main destinations can be divided into a number of overlapping types:

- Coastal, e.g. Costa del Sol, Blackpool;
- Scenic landscapes, e.g. south west Ireland, Scotland;
- Mountain and ski-ing, e.g. Alpine resorts, Nepal;
- City breaks, e.g. Paris, Cairo;
- Business centres, e.g. Korpilampi near Helsinki;
- Developing countries, e.g. South Africa, Kenya;
- Game reserves, e.g. Kruger National Park.

There are many benefits that tourism brings: employment, foreign currency, investment and the provision of services and facilities. However, it has also had a negative effect on many countries – not just economically but in terms of social effects and environmental damage. In some cases the destructive forces of tourism have destroyed the very attraction that visitors sought. Footpath erosion is a widespread process: repair of the Pennine Way will cost £3 million. Partly in response to these results there has been an increased awareness of the need for tourism to be managed so that tourist attractions and host communities are not destroyed by the impact of tourism.

Benefits to the environment	■ Safeguarding the resource for the benefit of future generations ■ The protection and enhancement of the special landscapes and features which together form much of the appeal to visitors
Benefits to the community	■ Real opportunities for community involvement in tourism and the creation of a better climate for development ■ Supporting the local economy and local services – for instance helping to support local transport systems in rural areas ■ Creating new business opportunities
Benefits to the tourism industry	■ Economic benefits for operators – for example, reducing energy bills by as much as 20 per cent by installing efficient insulation, and spending less on consumables such as paper and plastic goods by choosing reusable containers, washable table linen etc. ■ Better working relationship with the local community ■ Enhanced appeal for visitors from those market areas which have a high proportion of discerning and ecologically aware consumers, for example North European countries ■ Opportunities for the development and promotion of environment-friendly activity tourism such as cycling, walking, birdwatching, many water-based activities, and newer interests including conservation holidays
Benefits for the visitor	■ The development of quality tourism service ■ Better relationships with the local community ■ Closer involvement with and better understanding of both the people and the holiday destination

FIGURE 6.1 Sustainable tourism – the benefits

FIGURE 6.2 Making
tourism sustainable

If it is a proposed development, ask yourself:
Is it in the right place, or would it be visually more acceptable elsewhere?
Might it damage or destroy valuable habitats or archaeological sites?
Is the design appropriate to the location?
■ Consider the importance of reflecting the local style both inside and outside.
Is the scale of the proposals in keeping with its surroundings?
■ Could it be better landscaped? Is the development the right size and shape?
Are the specified materials the most appropriate for the project?
■ Use local stone, slate and wood if possible. How can you enhance insulating materials?
Has full consideration been given to all ancillary services?
■ What additional features, e.g. access roads, sewerage and waste disposal, will be needed.
If it is an existing operation, ask yourself:
Is the business being run in a sustainable manner?
■ Consider an environmental audit of the operation. Is there scope for new environment-friendly
technology, e.g. electric vehicles and solar heating?
Is it damaging the local or wider environment in any way?
■ Is it inadvertently polluting a water course or burning harmful plastics? Are the waste and sewage
disposal methods the most effective?
Are the suppliers environmentally friendly?
■ Do they recycle, save energy, avoid unnecessary waste or use materials from sustainable sources?
What is the relationship between the business and the local community?
■ Employ local people where possible. Use local shops and services and encourage your visitors to do
the same. Look at the potential for group purchasing of goods. Link your business to local community
and environmental projects and organisations.
Is the operation efficient?
■ How much energy could you save? Regular maintenance of energy-consuming appliances and
equipment can reduce energy consumption and fuel bills. Install energy and temperature controls in all
rooms.
Is it generating unnecessary waste?
■ Economise on the amount of waste water by installing more efficient washing machines. Use
phosphate-free detergents. Organic waste could be composted.
Can the use of disposable goods be reduced?
■ Use goods that can be used more than once.
Can more be done to recycle material?
■ Install recycling procedures
Can more be done to promote the business's environmental credentials?
■ Consider cooperative marketing with other environment-friendly operators. Tell visitors what you
are doing.
Are visitors being informed about the area and the community?
■ Provide visitors with advance information and advice about the area, local customs, traditions and
other areas.
Does the development have new opportunities for tourism?
■ Explore the potential for introducing creative, cultural, nature study and environmental holiday
activities.

6.2   Sustainable tourism

Sustainable tourism ranges from the prevention of long-term damage to the development of a sustainable local economy. It includes all forms of tourism development, management, and activity which maintain the environmental, social and economic well being of natural, built and cultural resources.

In *Tourism and the Environment: Maintaining the balance* the English Tourist Board and the Department of Employment argued that sustainability was the key to a more productive relationship between three key elements: the place, the host community and the visitor. It said it was 'looking to achieve a situation which can be maintained without depleting the resource, cheating the visitor or exploiting the local population'.

It listed seven principles for sustainable tourism:
1 The environment has a value for future generations. This must not be sacrificed for short term benefits connected with tourism.

2 Tourism is a positive activity, which can benefit the community and place as well as the visitor.

3 Tourism must not be allowed to damage the environment or threaten its future enjoyment. The relationship between tourism and the environment is a very delicate one and must be managed for long-term stability.

4 Tourist activities and developments should respect the scale, nature and character of the area in which they are found.

5 In any location, the needs of the visitor, the place and the host community must be reconciled.

6 Change is inevitable. Adapting to change, however, should be not at the expense of any of these principals.

7 Cooperation between interested parties is essential to achieve sustainable tourism.

The place

Carrying capacity is the number of visitors a place can hold before it suffers irreparable damage. This is determined by the location and size of the site, the nature of the activity and the fragility of the environment. Many sites around the world have suffered physical damage. Various measures have been used to combat the problem, including the closing of fragile areas, either temporarily or permanently; the introduction of entry charges or advance booking; or the staggering of times at which visitors are allowed to access the area or site. These are examined in the following case studies. Many attractions now use visitor centres to help with information interpretation and education about the place being visited.

The local community

Sustainability in rural projects is highly dependent on the participation of local people. Participation is especially important where a new tourist development is being created, or a new strategy being devised to cope with an unacceptably high number of visitors coming into the area. Moreover, tourism can be a positive force in creating jobs for local people. In Fermanagh, Northern Ireland, 70 per cent of the population live in rural areas and tourism accounts for 22 per cent of employment, the second most important part of the economy. A number of organisations and interest groups are active at a local/community level, many of which are engaged in preservation of their local culture and also the economic and social regeneration of the area.

FIGURE 6.3 Tourist related congestion in Stratford upon Avon

The visitor

Whether as individuals or in groups, the attitude of the tourists both to the place they are visiting and to the people who live and work there is crucial if sustainable tourism is to be achieved. For example the Lake District has 20 million visits a year, the North York Moors and Snowdonia 11 million and the Yorkshire Dales 7.5 million. Between them the parks have a resident population of about one-quarter of a million. On a busy Sunday afternoon, up to 2000 people per hour may cross the stepping stones at Dovedale.

The following case studies examine the main issues in sustainable tourism in contrasting areas, i.e. an undeveloped tourist region (Northern Ireland), a tourism-centred place (Killarney) and an expanding tourist market in a developing country, South Africa. It provides a variety of responses ranging from careful management to visitor exclusion.

Student Activity 6.1

1 How does sustainable tourism differ from mainstream tourism?

2 What are the main advantages of sustainable development for national parks?

3 Which groups, if any, might be against sustainable tourism in national parks. Explain your answer.

4 In what ways does the impact of tourists in places such as the Lake District, the Yorkshire Dales and the Peak District limit sustainable development in the English national parks?

6.3 Sustainable tourism in Northern Ireland

Tourism in Northern Ireland has considerable advantages in the area of sustainability. There is a variety of natural resources such as the Giant's Causeway, cultural heritage such as Carrickfergus Castle and industrial attractions such as the Bushmills Distillery and Belleek Pottery but there is, as yet, a relatively low level of demand. The areas which experience the greatest levels of pressure are generally in the east and north of the region.

Tourism expenditure as a proportion of GDP has been estimated at 2.2 per cent. Employment in tourist related activities accounts for 28 700 jobs or 5 per cent of the total workforce. This compares with 6 per cent in the Republic. With 1.56 million visitors in 1995 the Northern Ireland tourist industry earned £214 million in addition to the £57 million from domestic spending. The number of people taking holidays in Northern Ireland has been greatly affected over the years by the levels of violence. However in 1995, during the temporary IRA ceasefire, 461 000 people took holidays in Northern Ireland. This is the first time since troubles started

in 1968 that tourist figures have risen above the pre-troubles high point of 378 000.

By contrast, in the Republic of Ireland there were about 3.5 million visitors annually (a tourist for every citizen). Over 90 000 are employed making it the republic's third most important industry, accounting for 7 per cent of GNP. Hence there is considerable scope for promoting the tourist industry in Northern Ireland and some estimates suggest as many as 30 000 new jobs could be created. The negative images created by the Troubles have deterred many people from visiting the country. A comparison with visitor tourism to the Republic of Ireland reveals that the discretionary market contributes approximately half of total visitor tourism, in contrast to 20 per cent in Northern Ireland.

Following the ceasefires of the IRA and Loyalist paramilitaries in 1994 the British and Irish governments marketed Ireland as a whole. The two governments aimed to attract 92 000 additional visitors in 1995 with a £6.8 million tourism

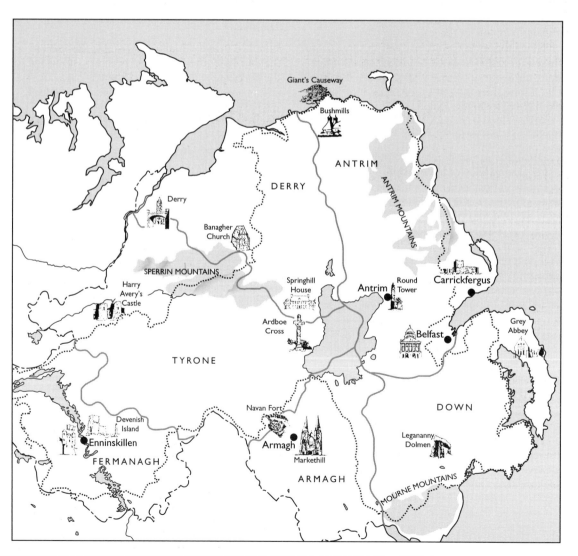

FIGURE 6.4 Sensitive tourist developments in Northern Ireland

incentive. A further £4 million was provided by the EU and the International Fund for Ireland. This provides a valuable opportunity to develop and implement sustainable tourism measures before significant problems arise. The ending of the IRA ceasefire in February 1996 had relatively little impact upon tourism in Northern Ireland. Between January and June 1996 visitor numbers were up two-thirds on same period in 1995. However, the violence that accompanied the Loyalist/Unionist (Protestant) marches throughout Northern Ireland, but especially at Drumcree in 1996 led to thousands of cancellations. Visitor numbers were down by between 40 and 50 per cent. Much of it was immediate reaction to the violence and most of the cancellations were from people from the Republic of Ireland. Tourism peaked in 1995 at 1.6 million, but fell 8 per cent in 1996.

Ironically, the 'troubles' of Northern Ireland between 1969 and 1994 have put Northern Ireland in a better position than anywhere else in the UK to adopt a sustainable approach to tourism. In 1993 the Northern Ireland Tourist Board (NITB) published the report *Tourism in Northern Ireland: A Sustainable Approach*. The main development priorities were seen as:
■ relating tourism to the environment;
■ involving the local community;
■ the need to aim for quality;
■ the need for all parties working together.
Tourism is a people focused industry, and this is true for the visitor, those employed directly and indirectly in tourism and those who live in areas that are tourist attractions.

Sustainable tourism need not be at odds with economic growth, as long as that growth is not at the expense of the environment. It is not a narrow specialist niche market, nor an idealistic goal. It is an attitude and approach which influences all aspects of tourism. Moreover, there are a number of benefits of sustainable tourism, to the environment, the community, the tourist industry and the tourist (Figure 6.1).

There are a number of examples of sensitive tourist developments (Figure 6.3). At Navan Hill Fort, the ancient seat of the Ulster kings, a purpose-built and carefully landscaped visitor centre provides a historical account of the fort. A visitor management scheme allows the number of people using the centre to be controlled. In the Slieve Croob area small low-key self-catering holiday homes have been built using derelict buildings. At the Giant's Causeway, renowned for basaltic rock formations, pressure is very severe. The visitor centre and footpath network were planned to manage people around the site and to keep the number of visitors to the most sensitive areas down. Although more than 370 000 people visit the Giant's Causeway each year, less than 10 per cent explore the entire site.

Some developments in tourism are quite substantial and reflect the growing confidence of investors in the province. Hilton International, for example, plans to build a £17 million luxury hotel along the Lagan River in Belfast. The Belfast Hilton will be part of a £130 million investment scheme in the Laganbank development site just 500 m from City Hall and the main shopping centre. This scheme will include a £29 million 2250 seat concert hall and conference centre and almost 500 000 sq ft of new office space, as well as restaurants and public houses.

According to the Northern Ireland Tourist Board Development Strategy (1994) there are a number of key issues and development opportunities. These include:
■ outdoor activities which, if not properly managed, have the potential to exert significant pressure on fragile landscapes;
■ activity tourism where demand is forecast to grow significantly. Increasing concern over health and fitness has stimulated a demand from the 30–45 age groups while the continuing importance of environmental issues has generated an interest in the sphere of environmental education;
■ accommodation as a key component in the delivery of quality activity holidays;
■ short, one week or less, stays with a shift towards the off-peak season;
■ the increasing interest of the corporate sector as a significant component of the market has implications for the type of facility on offer, as well as the level, type and standard of accommodation provided;
■ many activities which currently operate primarily for the benefit of the domestic leisure and recreation market and are relatively undeveloped for foreign tourists;
■ an increasing recognition of the mutually beneficial links between sport and tourism;
■ a growing recognition of the close relationship between tourism and the arts. The overall contribution of arts and culture to the Northern Ireland economy is being investigated by the Northern Ireland Economic Council;
■ festivals and events, entertainment, sightseeing, shopping and eating out as part of the increasing important special interest tourism product;
■ walking and cycling, horse riding, bird watching, golf, angling, boating, canals, language schools and genealogy as development priorities.

Student Activity 6.2

1 What are the attractions of Northern Ireland as a holiday location?
2 What advantages does Northern Ireland have over the Republic of Ireland as a tourist destination?
3 What role does sustainable tourism have in the development of the Northern Ireland economy?

6.4 *Sustainable development in Killarney National Park*

FIGURE 6.5 (right) The location of Killarney National Park, Republic of Ireland

Killarney is one of the most significant tourist destinations in the Republic of Ireland. Over 1 million visitors travel to County Kerry annually bringing an estimated £160 million into the area. The majority of these visit Killarney, which has a resident population of 7275 but over 8000 tourist bed spaces. The local economy is heavily dependent upon tourism. Consequently the Killarney National Park must continue to cater for the needs of the tourists by providing and maintaining the facilities necessary for visitor enjoyment. Conflicts between the environment and the economy have risen as has the number of visitors to Killarney. However, under Irish legislation where conflict arises between the needs of tourism and the needs of conservation, the protection of the natural heritage takes precedence over all other considerations.

FIGURE 6.5 (right) The location of Killarney National Park, Republic of Ireland

Killarney National Park

Killarney National Park (Figure 6.5) is included in the United Nations List of National Parks and Equivalent Reserves and has been designated a Biosphere Reserve by UNESCO. In the Republic of Ireland National Parks are defined as areas which 'exist to conserve natural plant and animal communities and scenic landscapes which are both extensive and of national importance and, under conditions compatible with that purpose, to enable the public to visit and appreciate them'.

FIGURE 6.6 (below) The four zone management plan in Killarney National Park

The five basic objectives for the National Park are:
- to conserve nature;
- to conserve other significant features and qualities;
- to encourage public appreciation of the heritage and the need for conservation;
- to develop a harmonious relationship between the Park and the community;
- to enable the Park to contribute to science through environmental monitoring and research.
Of these, nature conservation takes precedence over the others should any conflict arise.

Management strategy

Nevertheless, Killarney National Park is not without its problems. It does not comprise a self-contained ecological unit, consequently it is influenced by changes and developments which take place in the surrounding area. To successfully manage the interests of conservation and tourism Killarney National Park has developed a management plan, in which land use is controlled and conflicting uses are compromised.

The Killarney National Park Management Plan identifies four zones (Figure 6.6):
- Natural Zone: where nature conservation is the primary objective;
- Cultural Zone: where the primary objective is the conservation of noteworthy features resulting from human activities including demesne landscapes, archaeological and historic sites, buildings and structures;

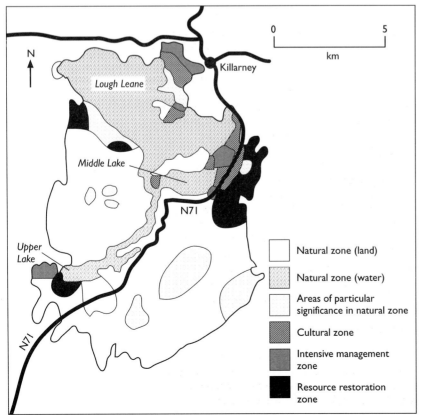

Natural zone (land)

Natural zone (water)

Areas of particular significance in natural zone

Cultural zone

Intensive management zone

Resource restoration zone

- Intensive Management Zone: where basic park objectives other than conservation are emphasised, provided park resources are not adversely affected;
- Resource Restoration Zone: comprising conifer plantations mainly in the Muckross area.

In addition, the Management Plan identifies a potential Buffer Zone around the Park within which development and change will be influenced in a positive manner. This has been developed in consultation with Kerry County Council, Killarney Urban District Council and other relevant bodies. Killarney National Park has a completely different problem to that of similar areas in Northern Ireland – it is over-used. Because it has been developed as a tourism centre for over a century, it has evolved a management plan which focuses primarily on the preservation of natural features. However, this is often at odds with members of the local community, many of whom wish to exploit its potential further.

Student Activity 6.3

1 Using the information provided, and an atlas, describe and explain why you think Killarney is an important tourist location.
2 How important do you think tourism is in the local economy? Give reasons for your answer.
3 You are in charge of economic development of the town and its environs. Write a 200 word report outlining the reasons why tourism should be expanded in the Killarney region.
4 What problems might increased amounts of tourism have on the park?

6.5 Sustainable Tourism and ecotourism in LEDCs

- There has been an 11.4 per cent increase in the number of foreign tourists to South Africa in 1995
- Over £3 billion was spent in 1995 upgrading the tourist infrastructure
- The proportion of people using South Africa for a holiday is increasing
- In 1995 approximately 800 000 foreign visitors went to South Africa
- The contribution of tourism to GNP will rise to 6 per cent by the year 2000

Tourists are attracted to developing countries, such as South Africa for a number of reasons:
- its rich and varied wildlife and world famous game reserves such as Kruger National Park;
- a tropical climate, especially in December–January;
- glorious beaches in Natal;
- cultural heritage and tradition of the Zulu and Xhosa;
- it is cheap compared to developed countries;
- English is widely spoken and there are many links with the UK;
- it is perceived as a relatively safe destination since the election of the new government.

There are a number of benefits that tourism can bring to a developing economy:
- foreign currency: the number of foreign tourists to South Africa has increased by 15 per cent per annum during the 1990s and contributes 3.2 per cent of South Africa's GDP;
- employment: thousands are employed in formal (registered) and informal (unregistered) occupations ranging from tour operators to cleaners and souvenir hawkers;

- it is a more profitable way to use semi-arid grassland: estimates of the annual returns per hectare of land range from R60–80 for pastoralism to R250 for dry-land farming and R1000 for game parks and tourism;
- investment: over R5 billion was invested in South Africa's tourist infrastructure in 1995 upgrading hotels, airlines, car rental fleets, roads, etc.

However, there are a number of problems that have arisen as a result of the tourist industry. Undue pressure on natural ecosystems has led to soil erosion, litter pollution, and a decline in animal numbers. Much tourist-related employment is unskilled, seasonal, part-time, poorly paid and lacking any rights for the workers. Moreover, resources are spent on providing for tourists while local people may have to go without. In addition, a large proportion of profits go to overseas companies, tour operators, hotel chains etc. Crime is increasingly directed at tourists; much is petty crime but there have been serious incidents, e.g. rape. Tourism is by nature very unpredictable, varying with the strength of the economy, cost, safety, alternative opportunities, stage in the family life-cycle and political stability. However, the tourist infrastructure is already showing the signs of strain: check-in queues lengthen, flights are over-booked, car hire companies are turning business away and hotels are running at almost capacity.

Ecotourism

Ecotourism refers to any form of tourism where the primary attraction is an ecosystem, such as a game reserve, coral reef, mountain or forest park. It has recently been widened to include 'primitive' indigenous people. It is widely perceived as the

FIGURE 6.7 (left) Recent trends in tourism in South Africa

acceptable form of tourism and that it is a form of sustainable development. However, much of that passes for ecotourism is merely an expensive package holiday that has been cleverly marketed with the 'eco' label.

Ecotourism developed as a form of specialised, flexible tourism. It emerged because mass tourism was seen as having a negative impact upon natural and social environments and also because there was a growing number of wealthy tourists dissatisfied with package holidays. In the original sense, people who took an 'ecotourism' holiday were prepared to accept quite simple accommodation and facilities. This is sustainable and has little effect upon the environment. However, as a location becomes more popular and marketed more, the number of tourists increases causing more accommodation and improved facilities to be built, e.g. more hotels with showers, baths and air conditioning, bars, sewage facilities etc. This is an unsustainable form of ecotourism as it destroys part of the environment and/or culture that visitors choose to visit.

South Africa has many attractions for tourists interested in ecology (Figure 6.8). The most famous and most popular is the Kruger National Park, established in 1926. The park contains nine rivers and has an unparalleled diversity of wildlife. It has more species than any other park on the African continent owing to its variety of habitats. All of the 'magnificent seven' species, elephant, lion, leopard, buffalo, cheetah, wild dog and rhino are present in the park. Vegetation is mostly bushveld and varies from park like areas, dominated by grass, to thick bush.

The climate in the Kruger National Park is sub-tropical with rains concentrated in summer between October and March. Winter is therefore a popular time to view game, as the vegetation is less dense. Surface water is restricted to rivers and water holes, and so animals must use these to find water. Consequently, there is a concentration of animals and tourists in specific places at certain times, i.e. around water sources during the dry season.

There are a number of potential problems that can result owing to pressures from tourists. There is an obvious conflict of interest between increasing the number of tourists in order to increase tourist revenue and the increased pressures on land. At best these can be considered as 'ecological headaches' at worst 'ecological nightmares'. These include population pressure, fire, soil erosion, vegetation removal, feeding and/or frightening the animals, air pollution and litter.

Management policies

The Timbavati group of unfenced game reserves in the eastern Transvaal, the Sabi-Sand reserves to the south and Klaserie to the north, together provide a buffer zone between the Kruger National Park and the farmland nearby. This is an important example of land use management as it eases the pressures on the borders of the park, especially from poachers and the gradual growth and encroachment of farmland.

In Kruger the main way of limiting the damage done by tourists is by limiting the number of tourists that stay there. This is achieved through the booking system for overnight accommodation, whether in chalets, huts or campsites. Facilities are comfortable but not excessive: for example, there is only one swimming pool in the park and there are no plans to build any more.

One of the major threats to the area is that of fire. Fire occurs naturally in the dry season and is important for the growth of new grass and the removal of weeds. However, it poses a threat to tourists and tourist facilities. Hence park authorities must manage fires. If they prevent fires the ecology of the area changes, as weeds invade areas and replace natural grasses. Hence, fires are lit and managed in order to create the natural conditions of a fire but in a controlled situation.

Soil erosion and vegetation removal go hand in hand. They occur as a result of increased pressures by people and vehicles on vegetation that is unable to cope. Normally, this occurs at specific pressure points around water holes and accessible river sites. Limiting numbers and shutting off roads is really the only option in this case.

FIGURE 6.8 Species diversity in the Kruger National Park

- 300 types of trees
- 49 species of fish
- 33 types of amphibians
- 114 species of reptiles
- 507 species of birds
- 147 species of mammals

FIGURE 6.9 National Parks and game reserves of South Africa

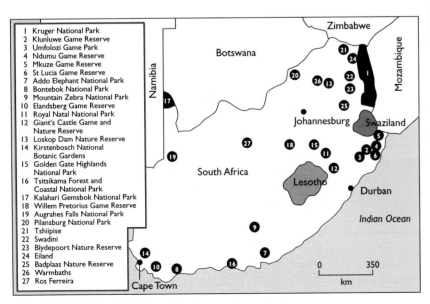

1 Kruger National Park
2 Klunluwe Game Reserve
3 Umfolozi Game Park
4 Ndumu Game Reserve
5 Mkuze Game Reserve
6 St Lucia Game Reserve
7 Addo Elephant National Park
8 Bontebok National Park
9 Mountain Zebra National Park
10 Elandsberg Game Reserve
11 Royal Natal National Park
12 Giant's Castle Game and Nature Reserve
13 Loskop Dam Nature Reserve
14 Kirstenbosch National Botanic Gardens
15 Golden Gate Highlands National Park
16 Tsitsikama Forest and Coastal National Park
17 Kalahari Gemsbok National Park
18 Willem Pretorius Game Reserve
19 Augrabies Falls National Park
20 Pilansburg National Park
21 Tshiipise
22 Swadini
23 Blydepoort Nature Reserve
24 Eiland
25 Badplaas Nature Reserve
26 Warmbaths
27 Ros Ferreira

Student Activity 6.4

1 Why is South Africa's tourist industry expanding rapidly whereas others, such as Egypt's, Kenya's and Sierra Leone's, are not?

2 With examples from an area, or areas, that you have studied, examine the problems of reconciling the needs of tourists, local residents, town planners and park managers.

3 What conflicts might arise, in an area such as Kruger National Park, between tourists and (i) conservationists, and (ii) farmers in the nearby areas who wish to expand their farming activities.

7
GLOBAL ECOSYSTEMS

7.1 *Introduction*

In every chapter of this book we have linked the concept of sustainability to a geographic system (population, urbanisation, rural areas, economic activities, tourism). This chapter looks at the concept of sustainability through the concept of an ecosystem.

It might be useful here to define some key terms:

■ habitat – a particular set of biophysical conditions to which plants and animals are adapted;
■ community – the different plants and animals living together in a habitat;
■ ecosystem – a delicately balanced system of complex interactions and relationships between plant and animal communities and their environment.

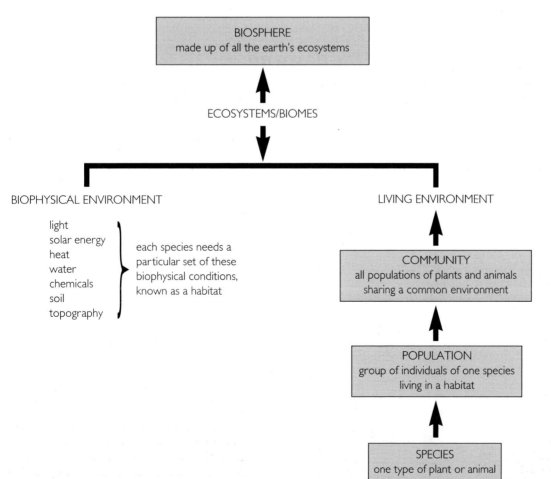

FIGURE 7.1 Components of the biosphere

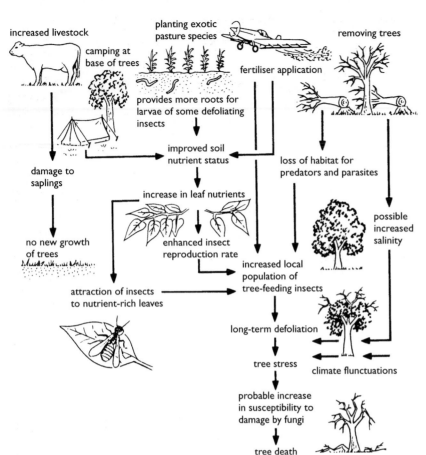

increased livestock

planting exotic pasture species

removing trees

camping at base of trees

fertiliser application

provides more roots for larvae of some defoliating insects

improved soil nutrient status

loss of habitat for predators and parasites

damage to saplings

increase in leaf nutrients

possible increased salinity

no new growth of trees

enhanced insect reproduction rate

attraction of insects to nutrient-rich leaves

increased local population of tree-feeding insects

long-term defoliation

tree stress

climate flunctuations

probable increase in susceptibility to damage by fungi

tree death

Figure 7.1 shows the components of the combination of ecosystems known as the biosphere. Figure 7.2 shows how the influence of man can disrupt ecosystems.

There are a number of global ecosystems currently under threat as a result of unsustainable development: the tropical rainforests, mangrove swamps, estuarine salt marshes and desertified savanna slopes. This chapter concentrates on a vast ecosystem often ignored in the literature of environmentalism: the world's oceans.

The world's oceans are often seen as an unlimited resource. They provide a source of plentiful protein in the form of fish and a seemingly bottomless sink for waste products from raw sewage to nuclear waste. The concept of *res communis* means the sea is often seen to be owned by everybody but managed by nobody. This results in problems. This chapter now deals with three ways in which man is disrupting the oceans' ecosystems:

■ overfishing;
■ whaling;
■ tourism.

FIGURE 7.2 How man disturbs ecosystems

7.2 *Overfishing*

The fishing industry represents one of the most dramatic examples of how man can quickly deplete a resource through unsustainable exploitation. World marine fish catches are declining. Many of the world's formerly productive fisheries are seriously depleted and some have collapsed due to overfishing. Figure 7.3 shows some of the threats brought on by excessive exploitation by modern fishing fleets and the degradation of natural habitats.

Plenty more fish in the sea

The phrase 'plenty more fish in the sea' encapsulates the common view of the sea as a limitless resource; but the sea's abundance is clearly overstretched:

■ the world's marine fish catch peaked in 1989 at 86 million tonnes, since then it has declined due to overfishing;
■ since 1950 the world's fish catch has increased almost five-fold;
■ in the past decade most of the developed world's fisheries have been over-exploited;

■ as stocks are fished out new species, previously ignored, are caught.

The fishing industry has grown twice as fast as the global catch and the result is over-exploitation. The huge industrial trawlers of the West are now heading for the waters of the Developing World. This is a serious threat not only to fish stocks but to the people themselves: the poorest two-thirds of the world's people get about 40 per cent of their protein from fish.

There are two main problems which affect the sustainability of fish stocks: new technology and the number of fishermen.

New technology

A vessel can now trawl nets where once it set only one; factory ships can freeze and process hundreds of tonnes of fish before returning to port; with cheap nylon filament, boats can set (albeit illegally) up to 65 km of gill-nets a day; mother ships can freeze and process hundreds of tonnes of fish before returning to port; spotter planes and helicopters search out fish; directional sonar let captains 'see' shoals of fish. Figure 7.3 summarises the effects of these new technologies. The conclusion is that there are just too many fishermen chasing too few fish.

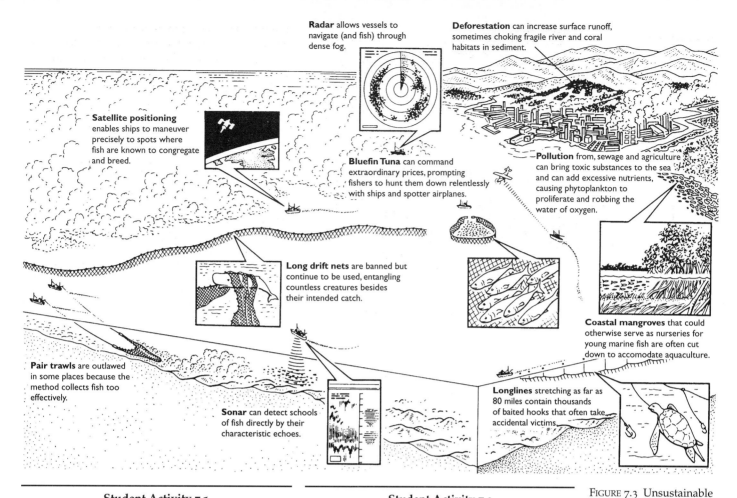

Satellite positioning enables ships to maneuver precisely to spots where fish are known to congregate and breed.

Radar allows vessels to navigate (and fish) through dense fog.

Deforestation can increase surface runoff, sometimes choking fragile river and coral habitats in sediment.

Bluefin Tuna can command extraordinary prices, prompting fishers to hunt them down relentlessly with ships and spotter airplanes.

Pollution from sewage and agriculture can bring toxic substances to the sea and can add excessive nutrients, causing phytoplankton to proliferate and robbing the water of oxygen.

Long drift nets are banned but continue to be used, entangling countless creatures besides their intended catch.

Coastal mangroves that could otherwise serve as nurseries for young marine fish are often cut down to accomodate aquaculture.

Pair trawls are outlawed in some places because the method collects fish too effectively.

Sonar can detect schools of fish directly by their characteristic echoes.

Longlines stretching as far as 80 miles contain thousands of baited hooks that often take accidental victims.

FIGURE 7.3 Unsustainable fishing, causes and effects

Student Activity 7.1

1 Use Figure 7.3 to construct a table identifying the causes and effects of man's impact on fishing stocks.

The European Union could cut their fleets by 40 per cent (Norway by two-thirds) and would still catch as much fish as they do today. In 1975 the Alaskan fleet enjoyed a season of Pacific halibut lasting 120 days – the fleet can take the entire catch in two 24-hour 'derbys' today. The Alaskan herring-roe fishery is open for a mere 40 minutes a year.

Too many fishermen

The contribution of fishing to the economy of most Western countries is minimal – less than 1 per cent in most cases – and it provides less jobs than most other sectors of the economy. Of far greater importance is its vital contribution to certain coastal communities. It provides jobs and incomes not just directly, but also in back-up industries like boatyards, processing, packaging and equipment suppliers. There are estimated to be around 300 000 full- and part-time fishermen in the EU. Given that most have access to the high-tech devices mentioned above the result is that fish stocks are becoming rapidly depleted.

Student Activity 7.2

1 Read the section on 'the Tragedy of the Commons' in Chapter One. Use this metaphor to discuss over-exploitation in the fishing industry.
2 'Too many fishermen, too few fish'. How far does this statement explain the problems of over-exploitation in the fishing industry?

FIGURE 7.4 Frozen Tuna at a fish market in Japan

Fisheries Management

There are a number of ways governments can encourage more sustainable use of fish stocks:

(i) Pay fishermen to give up fishing; harvesting the maximum sustainable yield might take only a fifth of today's fleet;

(ii) Fishermen should pay governments for fishing rights; when the Falkland Islands introduced charges of up to 28 per cent of the value of the catch, the island's GDP quadrupled and the number of fishermen decreased;

(iii) Restricting the right to fish by setting up quotas for the number of fish or the number of boats;

(iv) Give fishermen the rights to fisheries; only when fishermen believe that they are assured of a long-term and exclusive right to a fishery are they likely to manage it for the future.

■ where fish stay put (e.g. shellfish) governments can auction off chunks of the seabed.
■ where a whole fishery is controlled quotas could be traded to allow some fishermen to cash in and leave the sea.

Student Activity 7.3

1 There are four types of fisheries management given above. For each, outline an advantage and disadvantage of this type of scheme.
2 The environmentalist Sir Crispin Tickell recently made the following statement:
'We need to look at how it [Fisheries Management] can be tilted towards conservation of stocks and less towards who should have which bit.'
Do you agree with him? Explain your answer.

7.3 Saving the whale

… the whale once more rolled out into view; surging from side to side; spasmodically dilating and contracting his spout-hole, with sharp, cracking, agonised respirations. At last, gush after gush of clotted red gore, as if it had been the purple lees of red wine, shot into the frighted air; and falling back again, ran dripping down his motionless flanks into the sea. His heart had burst.

Moby Dick, Herman Melville

Moby Dick remains the most graphic of descriptions of whaling in English literature. Since Melville wrote the book in 1851 many whale species have been hunted close to extinction. As technology advanced, the dangers of hand held harpoons were replaced by the relative safety and detachment of harpoon cannons. The 1960s saw mass whale culls when more than 50 000 were killed every year. It represented one of the most obvious and repellent acts of unsustainable exploitation. By the 1980s the blue, humpback and fin whales had all been hunted close to extinction.

The result was a moratorium (an agreed suspension of activity) on whaling which was agreed in 1982 and came into force in 1986.

Threatened or not?

The moratorium is administered by the International Whaling Commission (IWC). It is a 'temporary measure'. The moratorium was meant to hold until stocks had recovered to an extent that hunting could resume without endangering stocks.

Figure 7.5 suggests stocks have recovered and this has seen environmentalists split into:
■ the environmental purists, like Greenpeace, who argue that killing even a single whale is morally wrong;
■ pragmatic environmentalists who warn that unless concessions are made to the pro-whaling nations of Norway, Iceland and Japan the IWF will splinter.
Figure 7.6 shows the strains on the moratorium. Iceland left the IWF in 1992 and Norway have threatened to do so every year since.

FIGURE 7.5 Current whale count

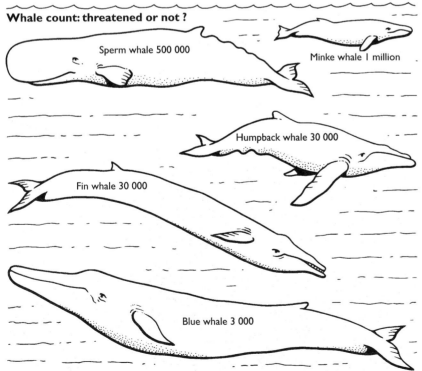

Whale count: threatened or not ?

Sperm whale 500 000

Minke whale 1 million

Humpback whale 30 000

Fin whale 30 000

Blue whale 3 000

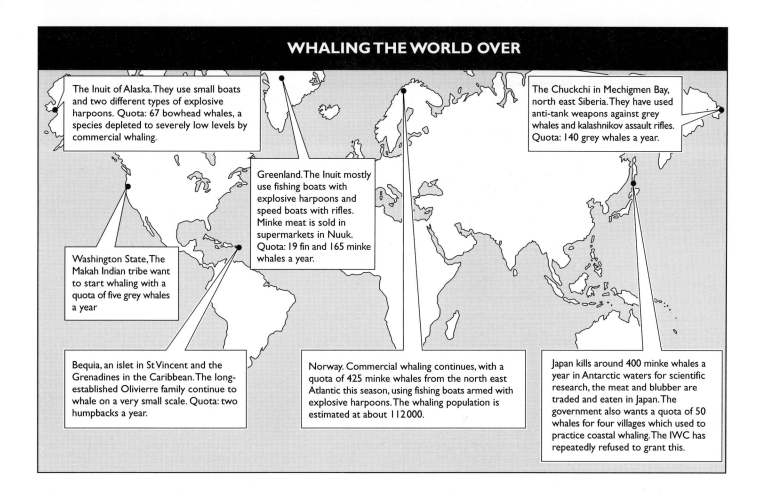

The Inuit of Alaska. They use small boats and two different types of explosive harpoons. Quota: 67 bowhead whales, a species depleted to severely low levels by commercial whaling.

The Chuckchi in Mechigmen Bay, north east Siberia. They have used anti-tank weapons against grey whales and kalashnikov assault rifles. Quota: 140 grey whales a year.

Greenland. The Inuit mostly use fishing boats with explosive harpoons and speed boats with rifles. Minke meat is sold in supermarkets in Nuuk. Quota: 19 fin and 165 minke whales a year.

Washington State, The Makah Indian tribe want to start whaling with a quota of five grey whales a year

Bequia, an islet in St Vincent and the Grenadines in the Caribbean. The long-established Olivierre family continue to whale on a very small scale. Quota: two humpbacks a year.

Norway. Commercial whaling continues, with a quota of 425 minke whales from the north east Atlantic this season, using fishing boats armed with explosive harpoons. The whaling population is estimated at about 112 000.

Japan kills around 400 minke whales a year in Antarctic waters for scientific research, the meat and blubber are traded and eaten in Japan. The government also wants a quota of 50 whales for four villages which used to practice coastal whaling. The IWC has repeatedly refused to grant this.

Student Activity 7.4

1 Figure 7.6 shows small quotas for local tribes in Siberia, Washington State, Greenland and St. Vincent.
  a Are the methods and extent of whaling similar within these groups?
  b Do you think such quotas are valid given these indigenous peoples' long history of hunting whales.
2 Quotas are much higher in Norway and Japan.
  a Japan kills its whales for 'scientific research'. Given the number killed (400) and the fact that meat is sold in Japan (a single Minke whale is worth £27 000) do you think this is valid?
  b The pro-whaling nations suggest a scientific model for 'sustainable whaling'. Should quotas be raised if the stocks have recovered?

Whale sanctuary

Anti-whaling nations are pushing for a whale sanctuary to help protect whales. The proposal is to ban whaling below 40 degrees south for at least 50 years (Figure 7.8). The sanctuary would remove the justification from Japan's 'scientific whaling' programme which is intended to monitor stocks ready for the resumption of whaling. The sanctuary follows findings by the UK and US officials that whales are worth more alive than dead.

Commercial whale watching has rapidly become a major tourist industry:
■ in 1993 about four million people went on whale watching trips;
■ this ecotourism has generated more than £200 million annually;
■ Japan is one of the world's fastest growing whale-watching nations.

FIGURE 7.6 Whaling quotas

FIGURE 7.7 Whale watching as a tourist attraction

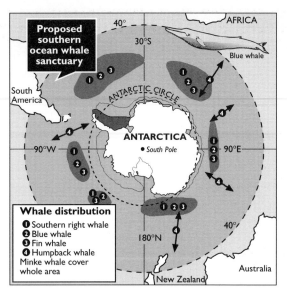

FIGURE 7.8 Proposed whale sanctuary

Whale distribution
❶ Southern right whale
❷ Blue whale
❸ Fin whale
❹ Humpback whale
Minke whale cover whole area

Student Activity 7.5

1 Does ecotourism represent a sustainable alternative to whaling?
2 Prepare a 500 word report to persuade fishermen to use their boats for tourism rather than whaling.

7.4   Coral reefs

Coral reefs are displaying signs of serious damage due to natural and human pressures. The reefs are found in shallow tropical saltwater (Figure 7.9). The coral reef is the world's most diverse and productive ecosystem. The slow growing polyps provide a habitat for fish, invertebrates and algae. Turtles and sea birds come to feed on the wide variety of fish, invertebrates and plants that live on them.

Limiting factors	Effects of limiting factors
■ Coral reefs grow in a very narrow range of environmental conditions ■ Temperatures need to be between 25° and 29°C ■ Water must be clear and shallow enough to permit adequate sunlight ■ Restricted to the areas between 30°N and 30°S ■ Coral is very slow-growing and fragile	■ inertia and resilience are low, slight changes in water temperature, turbidity (clearness of the water), amount of sediment in the water, nutrient and toxins can place the coral beyond the range of conditions in which it can survive ■ slightest contact with such things as anchors, feet or diving gear can weaken and break a section of reef ■ reefs are particularly vulnerable to the effects of storms and cyclones ■ temperature rise can lead to coral bleaching resulting in widespread mortality of reefs ■ the destructive crown-of-thorns starfish is a natural predator feeding on reefs

FIGURE 7.9 The coral reef ecosystem

Corals come in many forms and although rock-like in appearance, they are very fragile systems, vulnerable to damage and easily disturbed by both the natural environment and human activities.

They face threats from oil spills, the ornamental coral trade, global warming, pollution, smothering by silt, sewage and fertiliser run-off. Figure 7.10 gives some man-induced threats to coral reefs.

Tourism

Recent reports indicate that there is increasing poorly-managed recreational use of reef systems. Activities such as snorkelling, scuba diving and 'reef walking' (where tourists are taken on guided tours of shallow reef flats) play an increasing role in global reef degradation.

Diving

Studies have shown that well-used dive sites have considerably more broken and dead coral than less-used sites. Diving tourism can lead to damage in a number of ways:
■ accidental breakage of coral by collision with fins or tanks;
■ dragging consoles along the reef;
■ holding, standing or kneeling on the coral.
Damage is made worse by tour operators taking larger and less experienced groups. Cave diving leaves pockets of air which can kill roof dwelling fish and plants.

Reef walking

When people walk across reef they stir up large particulate sediment concentrations, equal to the maximum levels recorded during a cyclone. Trampling the reef has other effects:
■ coral growth rates are reduced
■ branching corals become replaced by short stocky ones
■ the corals become 'bruised' and look less attractive

Threat	Example
OVER-COLLECTING	
Fish	Futuna Island, France
Giant clams	Kadavu and islands, Fiji
Pearl oysters	Suwarrow Atoll, Cook Islands
Coral	Vanuatu
FISHING METHODS	
Dynamiting	Belau, USA
Breakage	Vava'u Group, Tonga ('tu'afeo')
Poison	Uvea Island, France
RECREATIONAL USE	
Tourism	Heron Island, Great Barrier Reef, Australia
Scuba diving	Hong Kong
Anchor damage	Molokini Islat, Hawaii, USA
SILTATION DUE TO EROSION FOLLOWING LAND CLEARANCE	
Fuelwood collection	Upolu Island, Western Samoa
Deforestation	Ishigakishima, Yaeyama-retto, Japan
COASTAL DEVELOPMENT	
Causeway construction	Canton Atoll, Kiribati
Sand mining	Moorea, French Polynesia
Roads and housing	Kenting National Park, Taiwan
Dredging	Johnston Island, Hawaii, USA
POLLUTION	
Oil spillage	Easter Island, Chile (1983)
Pesticide spillage	Nukunonu Atoll, New Zealand (1969)
Urban/industrial	Hong Kong
Thermal	Northwestern Guam, USA
Sewage	Micronesia
MILITARY	
Nuclear testing	Bikini Atoll, Marshall Islands (1946–58)
Conventional bombing	Kwajalein Atoll, Marshall Islands (1944)

FIGURE 7.10 Human induced threats to coral reefs

Tourist boats

Boats which bring divers to the reefs can also inflict damage. Dropping anchor on reefs can slice through coral and stir up clouds of sediment, choking the polyps. Repeated visits to same reefs and careless boaters who run aground compound the problems.

Reef curios

People who visit coral reefs often want a memento of their trip. This trade in reef curios is contributing to reef destruction. More attractive species of coral and shells are particularly vulnerable. This alters the complex food webs of the reef and reduces biodiversity. This in turn may alter nutrient flows and recycling.

Solutions

A number of organisations have been set up to address these problems:
■ the Professional Association of Diving Instructors (PADI) promotes Project AWARE (Aquatic World Awareness Responsibility and Education) which aims to teach divers to be more environmentally friendly;

■ in the UK, the Marine Conservation Society promotes the 'Let Coral Reefs Live' campaign with aims to reduce the curio trade and undertake conservation projects;
■ there is an international drive to set up permanent mooring buoys to reduce anchor damage.
In many ways economic reasons will determine the fate of coral reefs. Future revenues depend on sustainable use of the resource.

Pollution – Case Study: One Tree Island

Marine scientists in Australia have reassessed the effects that nitrate and phosphorus-based pollution has on coral reefs. The long held belief is that coral dies when nutrients from fertilisers and sewage run off the land; these promote the growth of algae which overwhelms coral polyps. Another cause suggested is the increase in fine particles suspended in the sea.

Tests on One Tree Island on Australia's Great Barrier Reef (Figure 7.11) added three times the natural levels of phosphorus to nine micro-atolls. Three atolls were kept as controls.

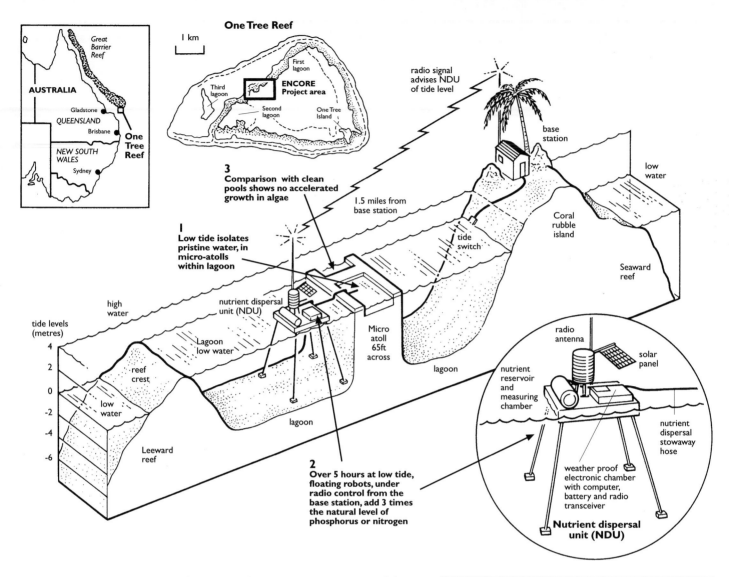

One Tree Reef

1 km

First lagoon

ENCORE Project area

Third lagoon

Second lagoon

One Tree Island

AUSTRALIA

Great Barrier Reef

QUEENSLAND

Gladstone

Brisbane

One Tree Reef

NEW SOUTH WALES

Sydney

radio signal advises NDU of tide level

base station

low water

3
Comparison with clean pools shows no accelerated growth in algae

1.5 miles from base station

Coral rubble island

tide switch

Seaward reef

1
Low tide isolates pristine water, in micro-atolls within lagoon

nutrient dispersal unit (NDU)

high water

tide levels (metres)

4
2
0
-2
-4
-6

Lagoon low water

reef crest

low water

lagoon

Leeward reef

lagoon

Micro atoll 65ft across

lagoon

2
Over 5 hours at low tide, floating robots, under radio control from the base station, add 3 times the natural level of phosphorus or nitrogen

radio antenna

solar panel

nutrient reservoir and measuring chamber

nutrient dispersal stowaway hose

weather proof electronic chamber with computer, battery and radio transceiver

Nutrient dispersal unit (NDU)

FIGURE 7.11 The tests carried out on One Tree Island

After 17 months scientists were surprised that algae were not growing faster in water enriched to 20 times normal levels. The findings stress the uncertainty involved in environmental issues. However, dumping pollution does have more serious effects on the reefs. The Australian researchers found:

■ coral growth was inhibited with a drop in their capacity to settle and develop new colonies;
■ reef animals suffered stunted growth;
■ coralline algae which 'glue' the reef together have their crystal growth poisoned.

Student Activity 7.6

1 In what ways might the economic interests of nations and businessmen which are at present disturbing coral reefs eventually lead to their conservation?
2 Use the example of One Tree Island to put the cases for and against limiting nitrate and phosphate pollution of coral reefs.

Index

Bibliography and Recommended Reading

Brandt, W., 1980 *North–South: a programme for survival*, Pan

Brundtland, 1987 See WCED

Brutsch, M., 1988 The role of the prickly pear in less-developed agriculture, *Ciskei Agriculture Journal*, 1, 7.

Chambers, R., 1983 *Rural development – putting the last first*, Longman

Dixon, C., 1991 Rural development in the Third World, Routledge

Elliot, J., 1994 *An introduction to sustainable development*, Routledge

Graven, E., et al., 1987 Essential oils – new crops for southern Africa, *Ciskei Agriculture Journal*, 1, 7.

Grigg, D., 1986 The world food problem, Blackwell

HMSO, 1995 *First steps – Local Agenda 21 in practice*, HMSO

HMSO, 1996 *Review of the potential effects of climatic change in the UK*, HMSO

Kirby, J., et al. (eds.), 1995 *The Earthscan reader in sustainable development*, Earthscan

Meadows, D. et al., 1972 *The limits to growth*, Pan

Meadows, D. et al., 1992 *Beyond the limits*, Earthscan

Nagle, G., 1995 Killarney National Park, *Geographical Magazine, 67*, May, 61–3

Nagle, G. & Spencer, K., 1996 *A Geography of the European Union*, Oxford University Press

Nagle, G. & Spencer, K., 1997 *Advanced Geography: revision handbook*, Oxford University Press

Nagle, G., 1995 What hope for Northern Ireland, *Geofile* 270

Northern Ireland Tourist Board, 1993 *Tourism in Northern Ireland: A Sustainable Approach*. NITB

Northern Ireland Tourist Board, 1994 *Tourism in Northern Ireland: A Development Strategy 1994–2000*. NITB

NRA, 1994 *Future water resources in the Thames Region: a strategy for sustainable management*, NRA

NRA, 1995 *Thames 21 – A planning perspective and a sustainable strategy for the Thames region*, NRA

NRA, 1995 *Policy and practice for the protection of groundwater*, NRA

NRA, 1996 *Upper Thames Catchment Management Plan: summary*, NRA

NRA, 1996 *Upper Thames Catchment Management Plan: Action Plan*, NRA

OFWAT, 1996 *Memorandum of evidence for the inquiry into water conservation and supply by the House of Commons Environment Committee*, OFWAT

Reid, D., 1995 *Sustainable development: an introductory guide*, Earthscan

Sarre, P. & Blunden, J., 1996 Environment, population and development, Open University

Van Heerden, I., 1987 The establishment of drought resistant fodder crops in Ciskei, *Ciskei Agriculture Journal*, 1, 6

WCED, 1987 *Our common future*, Oxford University Press

Zeisling, C., 1987 Rabbit production – a new alternative for Ciskei, *Ciskei Agriculture Journal*, 1, 7